Home

The Blueprints of Our Lives

Home

The Blueprints of Our Lives

To Michelle –
John Edwards

Edited by Former Senator

John Edwards

with Cate Edwards and Jonathan Prince

Collins
An Imprint of HarperCollinsPublishers

HarperCollins books may be purchased for educational, business, or sales promotional use. For information please write: Special Markets Department, HarperCollins Publishers, 10 East 53rd Street, New York, NY 10022.

All photos and illustrations are provided by each contributor, unless noted below: The illustration on page 9 by Eileen Prince and Tony Yin; the photograph on page 71 by Joy Lewallen; the photograph on page 72 by Senor McGuire; the photograph on page 93, courtesy of Audrey G. Wall; the photograph on pages 94-95 courtesy of the New Hanover County Public Library, Wilmington, N.C.; the illustration on page 147 by Jim Trippler; the illustration on page 151 by Donald Bruce Poynter; photographs on page 155 by Tierney Gearon.

Text on pages 50-53, taken from *In the Shadows of the Courthouse: Memoir of the 1940s Written as a Novel* by James R. Fisher, Ph.D.; Text on pages 86-87 © Francisco Jimenez.

FIRST EDITION

Designed by Howard Klein with K. C. Witherell

Library of Congress Cataloging-in-Publication Data has been applied for.

ISBN-10 0-06-088454-1
ISBN-13 978-0-06-088454-3

06 07 08 09 10 ❖ 10 9 8 7 6 5 4 3 2 1

{Contents

{Introduction}

My very first house was in Seneca, South Carolina. It was a small house in the mill village next to the factory where my mother's family had worked and not far from the mill where my father worked, constructed for workers like him by the company that owned the mill. When I was born, my parents didn't have very much—my father actually had to borrow fifty dollars to get my mother and me home from the hospital. But they both worked hard every single day to take care of each other, of me, and, later, my brother and sister—and that meant we moved around a lot when I was young.

My father didn't have a college education, so he had to take promotions wherever he could get them. We moved from mill town to mill town across the South until we settled for good in Robbins, North Carolina, when I was starting seventh grade. All that moving wasn't any fun—there's not a kid I've ever met who wants to change schools, say good-bye to friends, and start all over as the "new kid" again. But we made the best of it, because it was the only way for my father to move up in the mills.

Me, at nine months, in front of the housing project in Clemson.

The one house that sort of anchored us during that time was not our own house but my grandmother's house in Seneca. That's the house we all came back to. We spent countless hours there when we lived in Seneca, and we made countless visits back when we didn't. And when I went to college, I lived there with my grandmother and commuted to the campus in Clemson.

Probably because we moved around so much, for me home is more about all the things that turn a house into a home than it is about the house itself.

For me, home isn't the little two-bedroom brick house in Seneca on Mountain View Road; it's my mother crying in the kitchen as I leave for my first day of school and walk out to catch the bus. It's falling off my bicycle, breaking my two front teeth, and never doubting that my parents will fix me up.

It's not the housing project in Clemson. It's the comfort of

Me, age four, on the swing set,
in Seneca, South Carolina.

Me, at thirteen months,
in Union, South Carolina.

my mother making breakfast—eggs, bacon, and lots of biscuits with gravy, because biscuits are cheap but everyone will eat them.

It's not the house on a dirt road in Thompson, Georgia. It's my baby brother who almost died from pneumonia. Driving back and forth to the hospital thirty-five miles away in Augusta, the oxygen tent, my parents scared to death, and then all of us so relieved when he finally came home. It's the way my father would get furious at the big raccoon that would break open the milk bottles left by the milkman and drink the milk meant for our family. It's my grandfather, paralyzed on one side, sitting in his big chair next to the oil heater, watching Oral Roberts on TV, and praying along. It's my grandfather when I was older, now in a rest home, where I visited him every Saturday to cut his hair, to shave him, and just sit by his side.

It's coming home from football practice in Robbins around 6:00 PM and waiting for my father who would come home around 7:00 PM. It's sitting down to dinner every night, the whole family, with plates of fried chicken, vegetables, corn bread, meatloaf, and a glass of sweet tea.

It's going to work in the mill with my father in the summer, learning about the dignity of work side by side with the man who taught me about it by example.

It's my mother's job, my father's job, and my ball games; it's church on Sunday, church on Sunday night, and church on Wednesdays, too.

Home is family. Home is safety. Home is faith.

It's hard work with a purpose, love without measure, and the bond of generations. It's where children learn to navigate the challenges of our world, and parents seek to protect them from those challenges as long as they can.

Home. The place that helps to define how we see ourselves and how we choose to make our way in the world—the blueprint of our lives.

Where we learn to dream. Where we become who we are. And where we can always return. The A-frames and split-levels and mansions and ranches and apartments in this book are as different as the people who have lived in them. But this isn't a book about houses; it's a book about homes. About the values they rest on, the dreams they are filled with, and the people they have shaped.

The houses and circumstances are different, but much of what you find inside will be familiar. Much of what you find will be what you already know—that America at its best is a place of amazing opportunity, deep values, and unlimited optimism. That, given half a chance, we are a people who can accomplish anything. And that no matter where we come from or what we have done, our values are common and our dreams are shared.

These are our homes. This is America. Please come in.

—JOHN EDWARDS

{Jack Adair}

No matter how big we get, our roots always stay connected to our leaves. It is our roots, after all, that determine how the rest of us grows. Well, my life has been living proof that the apple never falls far from the tree. I was born in a small farmhouse out in Oklahoma's farm country. My father, Madison Bates Adair, and my grandfather Jesse Eugene Adair spent two years building with their own hands the house that Dad and Ma would move into when they were married in 1922. They would live there for the rest of their lives.

With three bedrooms, a living room, dining room, kitchen, screened-in back porch, and a big front porch, the simple house was all we needed. It sat in a valley, nestled between hills, a creek, and sprawling green pastures. We swam, fished, and sometimes bathed in the creek. We carried water from a nearby cold spring, where we also stored our milk and butter. To cook and heat the house, we relied on wood; for light, we used kerosene lamps. Since our farm was so remote, we hiked two and one-half miles to and from school every day.

Our family grew in that house; we grew taller, we grew older, and we grew closer. When you're eleven miles from the nearest town, the folks you live with are pretty much all you've got. And luckily for me, my family was a good one.

Even though we were poor, we were never hungry. The smell of Ma's bread cooking in the kitchen always crept through the house, making it warmer, and at suppertime we all gathered in my favorite room of the house, the dining room.

Even though it was quiet, we were never alone. And every night after supper, we used to gather around to hear Dad play the fiddle, and Ma would sing.

Even though it was simple, it was beautiful.

Growing up the way we did, out in the middle of nowhere and without a whole lot of spending money, you learn the meaning of hard work and self-sufficiency. I remember how hard the Depression hit, but we were very autonomous—raising livestock for our meat, milk, and eggs and growing our own vegetables. All of us contributed, and we relied on one another, trusted one another. I always found it funny how, miles away from our neighbors, we never felt isolated. In our little farming community, families understood one another and never hesitated to help out in time of need. I don't think we would have had that in a big city.

It wasn't until 1941 that we had electricity at the house, so that's when we added electric lights and got a radio and an electric iron. In 1946, after the war, we also bought a refrigerator

Back row, from left to right:
Me, Lois, Madison Bates, Jeanne, and Bob.
Front row: Karen.

and a washing machine. Even though we appreciated all this new, fancy equipment, sometimes we just preferred the simple life; in 1962, we put in modern bathroom facilities, but my dad still used the outhouse. We also drilled a well in the 1940s but still drew water from the old one for many years. I suppose we had just learned to make do with what we had and to trust it, and we didn't see the need for much more.

I lived in that house for twenty years, until I left to join the army in 1953. When I was discharged two years later, I took a wife and made a family of my own. Call me a simple man, but I loved the farm life. There were voices in those quiet hills that told me everything I needed to become a man. So once I became one, I decided to follow in the noble footsteps of my dad. We bought the farm from my parents in the 1970s before they passed away and built a home of our own on the property, not too far from the old house, where my sister still lives. I'm still on this quiet Piney, Oklahoma, farm today and, like my folks, don't plan to move out until I move on for the last time.

—JACK ADAIR, Farmer
Hometown: Piney, Oklahoma

Dutch, the family dog.

The house as it stands today, in Oklahoma.

{Noel Adams}

I suppose it's ironic that writing about my childhood home brings back memories of spending so much time outside of it, but its setting was the secret to its charm. The two-story house was built in 1858 on a 110-acre farm in southern Michigan. In 1948, after many years of being a tenant farmer, my father had finally saved up enough to buy this "new" house. A fifth grader at the time, I was so proud when I moved into a place we could call our own with my parents, sister, and two brothers.

Inside the house, Mom used to labor in the kitchen—pumping dishwater from the pitcher hand pump (our only indoor water), frying eggs on the stove in the morning, teaching me how to flip the pancakes for breakfast. The living room, where the big stove that heated the house in winter stood, was the family gathering spot. Here was where I sat listening to the radio and dreaming of far-off places to visit, reading a book I had checked out from the town library, or playing cards and checkers with my brothers and sister. In 1953, we got a TV, which brought me closer to the outside world that I had dreamed and read about. In the winter, after coming in from chores and milking the cows, I would cozy my backside up to the stove for warmth. The smell of wood smoke still reminds me of that stove as it was stoked. I also found that the best place to read on cold winter nights was wedged between the wall and the stove by the light of my grandmother's old reading lamp—which I've kept to this day.

Our house in southern Michigan.

But it was summer on the farm that I really loved, when we could stay outdoors forever. The summer sun allowed us to enjoy the best part of our "neighborhood," the St. Joseph River, where we found endless joy swimming and fishing in the stream and great adventure in the woods adjacent to its banks. Each night I slept on an old army cot on the screened-in porch, watching the fireflies in the front yard and reading a book under the covers by flashlight.

And as much as I detested the outhouse when nature called in the winter, I would happily stroll out there in the summer months, because that was where I could secretly roll my cigarettes after I took up my uncle's habit in my high school years. And I shared a wonderful outdoor space with my best friend, my mom—the vegetable garden. We would work together, and she would listen to me about anything and everything when no one else would.

My mother, Mabel Adams.

Even though we didn't have neighbors right next door, they felt very close. My grandparents lived within walking distance, and I spent a lot of time at their place. (Strange to think that my children have grown up with all of their cousins scattered across different states.) We also lived only about a mile from the six-hundred-person town of Tekonsha. An old-fashioned town even then, this was where all the farm families would gather on Saturday nights to shop and watch free movies in the park. The ultimate treat was a jelly roll at the bakery or an ice cream at the drugstore soda fountain (where I became a "soda jerk" in high school, pulling the levers to serve younger versions of myself).

After working for a year after high school, I left the farm in 1956 to attend college, but it was home until my parents passed away and my older brother took over. In that house, I built the foundation of who I became: knowing how hard we had worked to earn it and how precious it was to own it, learning enough to understand the value of education, and sharing meals with a loving family. I also took away from the farm a respect for nature, one of the small but important things in life that we're given for free. And those cold winters I spent ensconced between the stove and the wall gave me an appreciation of warmth, which brought me to where I am today—sunny California.

—NOEL ADAMS, Counselor
Hometown: Tekonsha, Michigan

{Isabel Allende}

I grew up in the house of my grandparents in Santiago, Chile, with my mother, two brothers, two bachelor uncles, and my grandfather. My grandmother died when I was very young but I remember her clearly—she was clairvoyant, funny, and loving. The house was built in the nineteen thirties by my grandfather and was demolished in the eighties. It was two stories with balconies, solid and stately. It must have been nice when my grandmother was alive, but after her death it felt large, ugly, and cold.

Santiago in the forties was a rather provincial town. Our neighborhood was upper-middle class, with large houses, big dogs, and children playing in the street. Every morning the maids would buy fresh bread; I can still remember the smell of that bread! At midmorning a mule-driven cart came selling milk and the maids would line up with their pots. There were street vendors selling all kinds of goods: from berries and goat cheese to vegetables, even brooms. A man who sharpened knives came by and an organ grinder with a tamed monkey dressed like a medieval page.

The family only gathered around the dining table on Sundays; otherwise we ate in the kitchen with the maids. My two brothers and I slept with my mother in a large bedroom, and at night she used to tell us stories. My favorite room in the house was the spooky basement, a forbidden place where I played imaginary games. There were rats and spiders in that basement, but I loved to hide there among discarded furniture and old books.

I was too lonely, sensitive, and imaginative to have a very happy childhood. I think that most of my writing is nurtured by the memories of my early childhood, especially my grandparents. My family was weird, so life in that house seemed interesting and a little crazy. My most striking memory of the house was of something that never existed: spirits. I could see them everywhere, and they made their way into my first novel, *The House of the Spirits*. One of my uncles collected books and I imagined that at night the characters escaped from the pages and roamed the house. I also thought the spirits summoned by my psychic grandmother still lived there. My nanny told me that the Devil was hiding in the armoires and that dead people were buried in the basement.

The house of my childhood does not exist anymore and it doesn't really matter how it looked in reality. What matters is the house that I invented. My granddaughter says that I remember what never happened. Maybe the house I remember never existed. I am sure it was not as large or as somber as I see it. I suppose that I created a place to fit my dreams and later recreated it as the setting for the stories in my books. I tend to enhance and change everything. I'm a fiction writer, after all.

—ISABEL ALLENDE, Author
Hometown: Santiago, Chile

An artist's interpretation of our home in Santiago, Chile.

{Hank Azaria}

I could see the whole Manhattan skyline from my bedroom window when I was growing up. My home was a three-bedroom apartment in the Forest Hills section of Queens—and that home was pointing me across the river from the very beginning.

Forest Hills was a really nice place to live. It split the difference between Long Island and Manhattan in many ways: architecturally, philosophically, geographically, and mentally. It was urban and suburban—and that was a good thing. Back in the '70s, Manhattan was a bit of a wild place; Forest Hills wasn't sheltered, but it wasn't scary—there was tons for a kid to explore, and little for a parent to worry about.

We lived on the fourteenth floor of a 25-story building—pretty big for Forest Hills back then. The apartment was pretty big, too; white tiles in the full kitchen, parquet floors in the dining room, and—God bless the shag years—a bright yellow shag rug in the living room. There was one bedroom for my parents, one for my sisters, and one for me. My sisters are ten and twelve years older than me, so by the time I was six or seven, they were both out of the house. I moved into the larger bedroom and pretty much had the run of the place (except when one of the adults was running me off to bed, which seemed to happen far too often for my taste).

When you live in an apartment and you don't have a yard, you've got to invent play areas wherever you can find them, and I invented all kinds of games in my room. The door to the terrace was my marbles campground. The wall of my bedroom was the back of Shea Stadium; I'd roll up a poster to make a bat and swing at a plastic golf ball—if it's this part of the wall you're out, but if it hits here, it's a double, and over here—that's a home run. And when the Knicks were playing, my Nerf hoop was both ends of Madison Square Garden. I would listen to Marv Albert call the plays, and I'd reenact them with my hoop. I'd be the Knicks when they had the ball, and their opponent when their opponent had possession. I'd keep my own score…and I'd try to skew the game for the Knicks. That way, even if the Knicks lost, they won in my game.

One whole wall of my room was a corkboard so I could put up whatever I wanted. The famous Farrah poster made an appearance for a while, and Bruce Springsteen and Walt Frasier were up there a whole lot. My friend Seth had put up wallpaper with lions and leopards so I put up wallpaper with lions and leopards—brown and yellow and gold. And—did I mention how lucky I was to grow up in the shag years? There was a big brown-and-yellow shag rug.

Me and my parents, with our apartment
building in the background.

But the two most important things in my room were the windows—one looked out to Manhattan, the other, my TV, looked into many different worlds.

I spent so much time staring out my window at the Manhattan skyline, just letting my imagination run wherever it wanted. My parents were big Broadway fans. They'd usually go alone, but every once in a while they'd take me. As I got older, I'd sit and stare out the window and follow the lights across the river to the theater district, imagining that maybe, someday, somehow, I could go there, and be on stage.

Home was a crowded house. There was always extended family coming over—aunts and uncles and cousins, watching sports or a movie, playing games, eating Chinese takeout or spaghetti dinners. A lot of laughter. People kidding each other, people laughing at the world. You know the classic Jewish sense of humor? No matter what, everyone was always laughing.

Except Hank. At least that's what it felt like sometimes. As I mentioned, I was so much younger, that I often got shooed off to bed. (It happened so often, that I've gotten pretty used to hearing people make noise in my house when I go to sleep; to this day, I don't really mind having people over and turning in before them—it almost sounds like home.) So I would lie in bed, listening to the sound of laughing grown-ups…and set off to find laughter of my own. With a little help from my grandmother.

My father's mother sort of spoiled us. She bought me my first TV when I was five years old —which was pretty unheard of in 1969. So when I got sent to bed, I'd take a nap and then I'd wake up and turn the TV on. I'd always look for something funny—Johnny Carson, Jerry Lewis, whatever. And I'd always get busted 'cause I'd laugh so hard my parents would hear me over the sound of the laughter out there.

Me and my TV in my room.

That's when, in some instinctive version of if-you-can't-beat-'em-join-'em, I started to do voices. I started doing Carson before I was six. I did Arte Johnson, "the little old man," from *Laugh-In*. Before I was ten, I had memorized comedy albums by Steve Martin, George Carlin, and Robert Klein. And I performed for the adults which, at least sometimes, meant I could stay up with them.

In New York, everyone is on top of each other—a great atmosphere when you're a mimic-in-training (so to speak). You hear every kind of accent, every nationality, every age, every pitch. And you take it in, and learn how to give it back. It started with my family. A lot of them are old world, from Greece and Spain, and it moved on quickly to my teachers. I had a Spanish teacher from Cuba, a history teacher from Hungary. At summer camp, I had soccer coaches from England and Scotland. And by the time I was acting, the voices of my youth were coming up from everywhere. I based characters in *The Birdcage* on Puerto Rican street queens; Moe from *The Simpsons* is a bartender that worked down the street; and the Dog Walker from *Mad About You* was the doorman from our building.

I was lucky to live in such a happy, exciting place, in a family that taught me that, no matter what, you can always laugh. And I was just as lucky to have my own little spot where I could go to get away and dream—my room, my TV, my window. When I think about my

Me in our living room, standing on our beloved yellow shag rug.

house, I think about my bedroom, about sitting at the window and staring across the river. That view anchored me—it defined my place in the world and it showed me where I wanted to go.

That skyline doesn't exist anymore—the World Trade Center was a big part of my view. When the terrorists attacked us on September 11, they took so much from so many. One of the things they took from me was any last, innocent notion that there is real permanence in the world. But what they can never take from me—what they can never take from any of us—is what I learned to do at that window. To stare out into the lights, to stare off into the future, and to imagine what we can make of it.

—HANK AZARIA, Actor
   Hometown: Queens, New York

{Mario Batali}

I spent so much time at my grandfather's farm that I feel like I grew up there. From the time that I was born in 1960 until I was fourteen years old, I visited all the time and sometimes stayed for weeks.

My great-grandfather, Antoine La Framboise, started building the farmhouse in 1897. He finished it in 1902 and brought my great-grandmother, Eugenie La Bissoniere, from Minnesota to Washington to marry her and move into it. My grandpa was born there. My mother, her sister, and her three brothers were all born there too.

Antoine was a jack-of-all-trades—a blacksmith, a wainscot, a farmer, and even a winemaker; he made Mass wine for local Catholic priests during Prohibition. And he was certainly a builder—not only did he build the farmhouse, he built the silo, the barn, the hop kiln, and a building that was the first community center in Moxee. For his blacksmith shop, he bought an old Protestant church on nearby Old Holland Road, moved it to the farm, and converted it to his shop.

And he definitely kept at everything he did til he felt he got it right—he experimented with many crops, from cotton to vegetables to tobacco, before finally settling on twenty-eight acres of hops and becoming one of the people responsible for making Moxee the hops capital of the world by 1930! The hops were grown on twelve-foot poles, handpicked by Indians at harvesttime, and then dried on burlap-covered slats in the hop kiln. And then, of course, they were sold to make beer.

Me and my Grandma after a home-cooked meal.

My grandpa really wanted to be a doctor, not a farmer, but fate and Antoine had their way. Antoine needed my grandpa's help on the farm, so that's what my grandpa gave him. He bought the farm from Antoine in about 1942 (for full market value; Antoine wasn't the type to cut anyone any breaks!) and farmed the hops until the 1970s, when he sold the house, farm buildings, and about three acres to my aunt Cherie and uncle Paul.

Our house was about fifteen minutes away in Yakima. I love Yakima. We had so much fun growing up there (this was the 1960s—think civil rights, Vietnam, and free love) that we still call it "Yakivegas" today. But the farm was special. It was an island of food, family, farming, and joy.

We'd drive up through the hop fields, and the first thing we'd see was this beautiful silo and the blacksmith shop. We'd bear right at the corner of the shop and park under a giant willow and then go into the house through the back door. The first thing you'd see—and smell—was the kitchen, with a big table in the middle and what always seemed like a million perfect snacks. The kitchen door led to the living and dining rooms, where there was a great big piano and a beautiful little vista looking out onto the front yard, filled with more willows covering the green lawn.

Me and my Grandpa.

Upstairs, over the kitchen, was Grandpa's den, filled with all the memorabilia of his times. He was a hunter and a fisherman—there was a cougar rug and stuffed animals he had killed himself on the walls. It was old world, important, and very private. It was my favorite room in the house. In the basement, there was a wine cellar dating back to Antoine's days as a winemaker. It's still there, undisturbed, with wooden racks for wine barrels and a dirt floor. There were owls in the barn and a loft in the silo. You could jump ten feet down from the loft into a bed of hay. It was kid-perfect.

We'd buy fresh vegetables at the farm stands in the lower Yakima valley and take them back to the farm to make antipasto and preserve it in glass jars. Even today, when I'm cooking in New York or anywhere else, I see my whole family together in the farmhouse kitchen, cleaning and prepping the baby onions, trimming the mushrooms, filling the jars.

As I get older, I realize how lucky I am to have known my grandparents so well and to have lived with them as closely as I did. That house is a bridge that spans Moxee and New York, my ancestry and my life today. It connects me to my roots in rural eastern Washington—my roots in the soil, in the earth, and in the whimsical world of growing things from which I draw my inspiration for my cooking in the big city of New York today.

—MARIO BATALI, Chef
Hometown: Yakima, Washington

My grandfather's
farm in Moxee,
Washington.

{Donna Brazile}

When I think of my childhood, I think of growing up along the banks of the Mississippi River in Louisiana. My dad, Lionel, and mama, Jean, were working-class folks who steeped their children in Louisiana culture. We were taught to believe strongly in God, respect others, whether neighbor or stranger, work hard without expecting a hand-out, and, above all, get a good education. "If you don't like what I say, just leave," my mother would say in a stern voice. We had no choice but to obey our parents. After all, it was their house.

My parents ran a strict household. They laid down the law, which they called "values" and we called "rules." Either way, we had plenty of them to live by daily. With so many kids, we learned by example. My parents were my role models. They were also our friends, and we called them by their first names, but we knew who was in charge.

We lived with my Grandma Francis, who owned the house where we lived in Kenner, on the Mississippi River just outside New Orleans. Back in the 1960s, Kenner had the feeling of a small town next to New Orleans, where my parents and all nine of their children were born. Our child-hood home had a simple structure. It was smaller than some of the houses around, but it was our home and we were proud to live there.

The two-bedroom wooden house was built in 1947 by my father's older brother, Ebbie, and his friends. Grandpa Louis had purchased the wood for the property from an old army barrack near New Orleans. Wood back then was cheap, and so was the land. Grandpa wanted to build a much larger house for his family of thirteen children (my dad was the baby), but he just couldn't afford to add on more rooms at the time. Instead, they built a little barn out back to raise poultry. Grandpa lived long enough to see some modest changes made to the house, including indoor plumbing and a bathroom by 1961. Until then, everyone used the bathroom out back near the barn.

The thing I remember most about our little wooden white house was its warmth. Grandpa placed little wall heaters in every room except the kitchen, which, with the stove and constant throngs of people, clearly didn't need one. Something was always stirring on the stove in our house. Grandma was an excellent cook, and mealtime was one of the most important times of day. Everyone gathered in the kitchen to eat Grandma Francis's delicious Cajun and Creole dishes, made from scratch. My favorite was chicken and rice smothered with crème corn, lettuce and tomatoes, and pickle salad. I don't recall ever skipping a meal, and if I did, Grandma would keep it warm in the oven until I got home.

There were two entrances to the house. Most people came in through the back door located in the alley we shared with my Aunt Ethel and her family. Once through the back door, guests landed in our nice-size kitchen, complete with modern stove, old-style icebox, and big wooden table where we all sat for meals.

Like most southern families, the kitchen was the center of our home. Our parents conducted business there between meals, and when that was happening, children were forbidden to play or even eavesdrop on the grown-ups' conversation. When neighbors dropped by, my mother or grandma would give them something to drink, like iced tea, lemonade, or a cold beer. Soon the chatter would begin, and I would look for ways to sneak in and hear the latest news or gossip. If Jean caught me walking near, she would holler, "Here comes tape recorder, better stop talking because Donna is recording." Truth was, I did not own a tape recorder, but I took careful notes of what was being said so I could ask questions later. There's no question, listening in on grown folks' conversations got me in a lot of trouble back on Filmore Street.

Our family home in Kenner, Louisiana.

DONNA BRAZILE

Now, we also had a front room facing the street. For official visits, Grandma would allow the front door to be used, where her guests would enter a cozy living room complete with a small box TV and record player. I witnessed these visits from far away since Grandma sealed off the living room to the kids. We were not allowed to sit on the sofa or the other furniture. When I was younger, it puzzled me that so many people barricaded their living rooms from members of their own family. They wrapped the furniture in tough plastic, as if to remind us not to touch anything in sight. When I got older, I figured out why the old folks cordoned off the front rooms: they couldn't afford to have us mess up or ruin the furniture because it took years to save up the money for these prizes.

We kids had our own space, though. Our den occupied the wide-open area leading to the kitchen and was a room where we could play and study. We had to keep it clean and respect others who shared the room with us, but we could sit on the furniture and even eat our nightly snacks in the den. During the summer months, we were allowed to sleep on the den floor with the windows open, and a huge fan was placed next to the front door to draw in fresh, cool air. I loved those moments because we got a chance to be together without any adults in the room. There, we could talk about our wildest dreams and what we wanted to do with our lives.

We also used those moments to talk about our friends in the neighborhood and what gossip we learned during the day. Most of the time, we just shared laughter about our neighbor Mrs. Eddie B's cooking, which was strange because she cooked wild game like possum. At times, we could smell the chitlins she made weekly, and we complained about the odor. Still, we spent lots of time out back just listening to her stories about life in Mississippi.

She and Mr. West (her husband) lived behind our home. They had a smaller shotgun double house attached by a single bedroom. The Conrads lived next door. We loved those neighbors, especially since they seemed so different. Mrs. Eddie B went fishing twice a week and sold her catch to all the neighbors. As a result of her passion for fishing, I was able to start a little bait and tackle shop. She was my only client, but it meant my parents had fresh fish like croakers, trout, and catfish twice a week and I had a little extra spending money.

With so many mouths to feed, my mother enjoyed buying seafood from her good friend and neighbor. Most of all, we loved listening to Mrs. Eddie B's accent. She was from Mississippi, and we never understood a word she said. "Would ya tell yo mama dat the fish is fresh today," as she spat out tobacco. "Yes, ma'am," we replied. We had a lot of laughs on Filmore Street. Our home was small, but the hearts inside were warm and full of joy. That is, until the weather changed.

Every year of my childhood, we braced for the "big one" or the storm that would not only pull down tree limbs, but also bring rain and wind damage that could cause havoc to our home.

Hurricane Katrina devastated much of the Gulf Coast in 2005, but there was a Big One before that. It came in 1965 when I was five years old.

Hurricane Betsy was her name. She was fierce. On the morning she was supposed to make landfall, we all sat in the den area listening to the radio for news. Everyone was scared. Lionel spent the day outside boarding up the windows, and Jean and Grandma made ham sandwiches with homemade buttermilk biscuits. Our parents told us to pray that the storm would take another path. We did, but it didn't matter. Hurricane Betsy was well on her way toward us. By the time she made landfall, we had lost most of the barn and half the roof. Our little house was severely damaged from the strong winds and torrential flooding when the storm surge toppled the levees.

Lionel took us out of the house, one by one, through the window and over to Aunt Ethel's. Jean was seven months pregnant with my little brother Kevin, and she was forced to leave as well. Only Grandma remained, inside her little room up front. She would not come with us. We begged her. She refused to leave her home. When the storm blew over and it was safe for us to go back to our home, we ran over to check on Grandma.

She was fine. The house was destroyed, but the one room still standing, almost intact, was her little room with a crucifix of Jesus right next to her bed. Grandma was sitting in her rocking chair, praying and looking out the window to see if everyone was all right.

That was the essence of my childhood—a time of enormous challenges, but a great time to be alive and conscious of your surroundings. My parents did not have great wealth or even own a car. We got by on faith and hard work, just as they predicted when we were growing up. Still, they gave us things money could never buy—good advice and strong leadership. By obeying their rules, we stayed the course. We went to school and on to college. They taught us daily to give back to others, especially those less fortunate. We did. This helped to shape not only my childhood, but my future, where I decided to devote my life to helping others and standing up for what's right.

Our little house remains intact despite the damaging winds and terrible flood that occurred during Katrina. Just as before, when the little wooden house was rebuilt after Hurricanes Betsy and, later, Camille, my family plans to patch it up, repaint it, and build again. My family is now living in temporary homes all over America. They desperately want to go home to rebuild their houses and community—better than before, but still in the same manner—one piece of wood at a time, borrowed from somewhere but strong enough to provide cover for the next generation of Braziles.

—DONNA BRAZILE, Political strategist and commentator
Hometown: Kenner, Louisiana

{Aggie Briscoe}

My grandparents' house was built around 1955 by my grandfather with help from friends and neighbors in the tradition of all farming families. Every Saturday, my mother would leave my brothers, sister, and me with our grandfather while she and my grandmother, whom we called Lil Mom, went grocery shopping. And we spent nights and weekends there on many occasions.

Lil Mom and Grandpa's house is situated a ways back from the main road that runs in front of the house. A dirt road led from the main road up to the house, and it got very muddy when it rained. Grandpa would always warn drivers to "stay out of the ruts!" I always thought that was funny because who would want to get stuck in the mud?!

I also remember how my brothers and I loved to run and jump off the front porch over Lil Mom's flowers. If we didn't make it and broke a flower, she'd threaten to make us pay her a million dollars for each flower we broke. Whenever I see flowers like the ones she had, I remember her.

There was a living room, three bedrooms, and a large kitchen, but my favorite room in the house was the so-called dining room. So-called, because there was never a dining room table in it and nobody really dined there, but I guess that was their intention when it was built and the name stuck. Instead, it was Grandpa's throne room. He'd sit in his recliner, watch TV, and hold court, commanding family affairs. Any child entering the house had to first greet him with, "Hello, Grandpa," shake his hand, and engage him in conversation until you were dismissed to see what kind of snack you could beg from Lil Mom or run out to play. Adults also had to greet him first upon entering the house. I later realized it was a sign of respect he demanded and received without question as head of the household and as a man.

Grandpa lost his sight for several years, but this ritual continued uninterrupted, although with an added challenge—Grandpa was determined to identify each person by his or her voice. I'll never forget how moved he was after his sight was restored and each grandchild walked up to him and greeted him in the usual manner. He was so happy to see all of us again and he cried. That memory will always be with me.

It's not surprising rice was the Friday meal. The most significant landmark in Raywood, Texas, is the rice dryer—not only because it is the tallest structure in the area, but also because of the impact rice had on the whole community. It was a rite of passage for young men to work a summer at the rice dryer. Girls were taught early how to pick out the rice husks and bits of debris from the sacks of rice our fathers and brothers brought home as part of their pay. As we grew older, we were taught how to cook the daily pot of rice to perfection.

Rice was grown across the road from the school, so we were always in tune with the whole process of growing and harvesting it even if we didn't consciously think about it. The seasons were marked by whatever was going on in the rice fields. In late winter, the fields were flooded in preparation for the planting. The bright green of the shoots in spring offered a beautiful sign of renewal. As summer progressed, the stalks turned golden

Lil Mom and Grandpa's home in Raywood, Texas.

brown, which meant that autumn and the harvest were near. Today, I live in an area of California where rice is grown, and when I drive by and smell the rice, it smells like home.

My cousins would visit every summer. Even though most of us lived only a few miles apart, it was cause for excitement and revelry. There'd be a big barbecue outside. The men would sit on the front porch and play dominoes or cards. We had the run of the area between the yard and the main road. Eventually a softball game would get started, and our parents would join in. Or maybe we'd play with the only croquet set in Raywood. The feeling of summer fun, family ties, and youthful joy will never leave any of us—we all got together for a fish fry reunion not too long ago, and we might as well have been teenagers again.

But Lil Mom and Grandpa's house wasn't only about fun and love. It was where I learned about respect. Remembering Grandpa on that throne of his, holding court in the center of the house, and remembering how his door was open to any family member who needed it, I learned how to earn respect—and how to give it in return.

—AGGIE BRISCOE, Information systems manager
Hometown: Raywood, Texas

{Mary Catherine Brouder}

My hometown is The Bronx, New York. Til I was seven, seven of us lived in a four-room apartment—my mom, my dad, my older sisters, Corina, Christina, and Cornelia, and my older brother, Cornelius, whom we've always called Neil.

Today, I'm a senior at Harvard, where I'm the arts editor of the *Harvard Crimson*; I also write for the *Irish Emigrant* newspaper and *Irish America Magazine*. So I know something about the "Five Ws."

Let me tell you, when seven people live together in a four-room apartment, home is all about the *who* and not so much about the *when, where,* or *what*. As for the *why*, you'd have to ask my mom and dad.

The only room that really mattered to all of us was the living room. It seemed like everything important that happened in our family happened there. Academics were not the most important aspect of our young lives, but we all had to do our homework, and we did it together around the dining room table—which was in the living room.

There was never a strict bedtime, and we always seemed to have company: neighbors, relatives, or friends sitting around, telling stories—in the living room. The kettle was always on, and it seemed food was always being served—in the living room.

Shortly before I was born, my sister Christina was run over by a drunk teenage driver right

Our apartment building in The Bronx, New York.

The Spirits of Gilbride.

outside our building. She was in the hospital for a very long time. When she came home, it was in a full body cast. She spent the next year in a wheelchair. My mother wanted to do something to give thanks for my sister's recovery. Everyone in my family was musical, so my mom decided to turn us into a musical group that would travel around the country and perform at hospitals and places like that.

So that's what we did. We became the Spirits of Gilbride. Guess where our first performance was? Of course. The living room.

And for the next eleven years we played more than a hundred shows a year in hospitals, nursing homes, and rehab centers all across the country. We've had the honor to play at the White House, Disney World, and Yankee Stadium (right at home in The Bronx!), as well as at places like Radio City, Carnegie Hall, and Lincoln Center.

We performed and practiced several times a week, we went on tour every summer…but as much as we loved life on the road, we loved getting back home to our living room.

Now that we're all grown up…well, I'm nineteen and finishing college; Neil is twenty and an artist with an engineering degree; Cornelia is a photographer with a law degree; Christina is a chef with a political science degree; and Corina is a singer with a nursing license…but the point is, we still get together and play music. And every time we do a show, it still seems like the five of us are back there, where it all started, in our living room.

—MARY CATHERINE BROUDER, College student
Hometown: The Bronx, New York

{Eldred Burgy}

My father hired a carpenter and began
construction of the house I grew up in during World War I. My father, mother, two brothers, and I moved in when it was finished, in 1918. My father died five years later, so this house holds almost all of my memories of our family together. A young five when we moved in and an old ten when we left, this large, two-story farmhouse is where I really grew up.

A coal furnace in the basement fueled the hot-water radiators that heated both floors. Often in the frigid Iowa winters, we would warm up by sitting on the radiators that were in every room or crawling under the kitchen stove—it was just high enough off the floor to avoid getting burned! As our mother prepared meals for us, the sounds of her cooking could be heard from the kitchen and aromas wafted through the house. We used a teakettle for hot water to wash our dishes and hands. My father would take some of the water to shave in the cloakroom, which was lined with wall hooks for hats and coats and a place for work boots. This was also the site of our only telephone, but you could hear it ring throughout the house. To use the telephone, we pulled down the receiver and earpiece and cranked the side handle to contact the operator. Because it was a party line to which anybody in the local community could listen, we had to be careful when using it or at least ask everyone to not remain on the line.

In the winter, I would watch the snow fall through our kitchen window in the back, sometimes piling up as deep as five or six feet between December and February. My brother Irvin and I had to shovel snow to clear the house walkway so that we could get to our farm chores. During the summer months, when the temperature got up to one hundred degrees, we lived in the five-room basement, where it was cooler. We stored wood for the stove down there, as well as corncobs and canned fruits and vegetables (tomatoes, apples, grapes, and rhubarb) that we helped our mother prepare. I had my own room on the second floor, as did my parents and brothers, but we all stayed in the middle room of the basement together during those scorching summer nights.

We lived only about three miles from Conroy, Iowa, an unincorporated rural town with a population of fewer than one hundred. The town basically consisted of a general store, bank, and Lutheran church. Our closest neighbors were five other family farms. We all helped one another during the fall harvest, with chores like cutting corn, oats, and hay that we'd then sell or feed to the hogs. During the winter, individual families hosted farm parties, the venue rotating from house to house. When it came our turn to host, groups would scatter about our house. The men played euchre in one room on the first floor, the women socialized in another, and the children played upstairs. All the children from the neighboring farms went to the same one-room schoolhouse, about a mile and half from our house. Like many of the children, my brother Irvin and I each carried our makeshift lunchboxes, one-gallon Kayo syrup cans with handles and lids (like paint cans), and walked to school.

Our farmhouse in Iowa.

Each night before bedtime, my mother read books like *Pilgrim's Progress* to us at the kitchen table for an hour. My father would also set up camp there to read the newspaper and mail. I loved the kitchen because its lighting and the warmth of the stove made it a natural place to gather and tell stories, and just enjoy one another. Our close family ties were formed and strengthened there, living on a farm where everyone depended on everyone else.

Our five years together came to an end when my father died in an automobile accident in 1922. My mother did not drive, and she could not take care of the farm by herself while raising three children. So, when I was ten years old, my mother, brothers, and I moved about ten miles away to Morengo, where we could attend grade school without depending on transportation. Most people drove around the area in Model-T Fords, but after my father died, we had use only of a horse and buggy and a wagon to visit Conroy and other communities. We kept the farm, and my mother leased it to another farmer. The farmhouse still stands on its original 112 acres and remains in our family, home now to my nephew and his family.

Today I am no longer able to visit the farmhouse because of my age and health, but I remember those early years when I learned the importance of maintaining close family ties throughout life. I had to grow up early with my father's death and assume the responsibility of helping my mother make difficult family decisions. My beloved wife of fifty-eight years passed on five years ago. Now my son and daughter help me live life each day, just as my mother helped me and I helped her in turn. It's wonderful to know that my mother's strength and love live on in our family.

—ELDRED BURGY, Retired intelligence analyst, Air Force and Defense Intelligence Agency
Hometown: Conroy, Iowa

{Robert Carr}

Most people know me as Robert Carr, but my Indian name is Guwatemo. I was born in July of 1940 on the Pueblo of Laguna Indian reservation in New Mexico, in the same village my parents and my seven brothers and sisters were born. Pueblo society was matrilineal, and one of its customs was that when a couple married, the husband would move in with his wife's family. So one of my first homes was my maternal grandmother's home. It wasn't the only one, though; until I turned twelve, I lived in three different, but very similar, houses. All of the buildings on the reservation were alike, in fact—one-story structures with floors of mud and straw, kerosene lamps for light, and no indoor plumbing.

One of these houses, my parents' house, was about 1,800 square feet, quite large by local standards. There was a small entry room and the kitchen held the all-important wood-burning stove for heating and cooking. Four other rooms were used for sleeping and storage, and a closet with a cellar underneath kept the staples that my parents purchased using their ration books during World War II. The kitchen stove was our only source of heat, but it really only warmed the kitchen; we lived at a very high elevation, so the rest of the house was freezing cold most of the time.

My grandmother's house was about the same size: a small kitchen with a wood burning stove, plus three additional rooms. Behind this house was a large cellar with bins that held grinding stones. The women in the family used these stones to grind corn; I can still see them, dressed in traditional Native American clothing, and singing in unison while they worked.

My parents' home in the village of Paguate, Pueblo of Laguna Indian Reservation.

My father tended sheep, so he wasn't usually found in these houses.

We saw my father often, though, at the third house, a sheep camp where the family stayed during the early spring of each year to lamb and shear our flock. This was a one-room house measuring about 10' x 15', with a wood-burning kitchen stove, a fireplace that we never used, and a large homemade table with benches. There was a makeshift cabinet that held the kitchenware, and against a wall was a bedroll for my parents, who slept on the floor. Children and whoever else was there helping with the flocks would sleep outside in the open on homemade mattresses or pelts. When my father's siblings consolidated their flocks for lambing and shearing, there could be fifteen people staying together. Given the ratio of people to space, the sheep camp house was mostly used for cooking, eating, and shelter from the wind and cold. After the lambing and shearing season, our father and the older children would take the flock to a higher elevation and greener pastures. The children returned home just before school started in mid-August.

Growing up on the reservation was very structured—our parents and our tribe had high expectations. From a very early age, we had chores to do before we were allowed to play—chopping wood, going for water from the village pump, hoeing in the garden. We learned that we should never have to be asked to help, nor should we expect to be paid. We were taught to respect our elders, and always to address them according to their relationship to us—Uncle, Brother, Grandfather.

It was a lot of work at the sheep camp, but we had fun, too. Every day we would compete to see who could find the most bird nests and arrowheads while herding. At the end of each day we'd gather at the kitchen table to show each other the arrowheads we found, each of us judging the legitimacy of the others' findings and tallying up the "credits." Some nights, we'd have pudding, made in a container lined with cornhusks, and everyone would want their share so they could chew the leftover pudding that had dried onto the husks.

The smells of pinto beans cooking on the stove, freshly baked bread from the outdoor oven, and fresh tortillas sifted through the house as my mother cooked. She never made a big deal of it; she never complained about all that she did for our family day after day, and nothing was easy. To wash our clothes, for example, she'd have to trek them down to the small creek that ran below the village.

Everyone worked hard, but after the work was done we relaxed and enjoyed each other's company. While my parents were quiet people, there always seemed to be a lot of conversation and laughter going on especially around mealtime. We were never embarrassed about making fun of ourselves. Both of my parents always seemed to be humming songs—my mother humming soft church hymns, my dad humming traditional songs translated into Keresan, our tribal dialect. In the winter, he would sit by the stove and sing and me and my younger brother would dance the traditional Pueblo deer dance.

While it was very rare that all eight children would be home at the same time, Christmas was often the exception. At midnight on Christmas Eve, traditional social dances were held at the village Catholic church. My parents rarely attended them, but we children always did. When we returned home, mother and father would be waiting with food on the table for us to eat before bed. This was the best part of Christmas—the reminder that our parents would always be there for us.

My parents had fourth and sixth grade educations. Their only income came from selling lambs and wool, and their vegetable gardens supplemented our food supply. But they managed to give us a good life and show us their love for each other and us in so many ways. They taught us about personal responsibility, primarily by the example they set. They shared responsibilities for our care, watching us in each other's absence. My fondest memories are of my father holding our hands as we herded sheep or my mother as we helped with household chores.

And they made sure we went to school. Despite their meager income, they sent us to a Presbyterian boarding school in Arizona instead of the government boarding school in Albuquerque. (There were no high schools on the Laguna reservation until the 1960s.) As we got older, we worked to pay our own way. Four of us eventually graduated from college, two with master's degrees.

My parents also taught us that life could be hard at times, but we could overcome whatever challenges we faced. They never let anything get in the way of giving their children a stable and loving environment, teaching us that we were always worthy and always capable.

When I was eighteen years old, I traveled by train to begin my freshman year at a small Midwestern college. I slept through my stop and ended up in Topeka, Kansas, where I got off the train and went to eat breakfast at a local diner. They told me I couldn't be served. And in that moment, I realized what a profound impact my parents had had on me. I wasn't scared; I didn't want to run back to the safety and security of the reservation. I thought of my parents, of what they would do, and what they would expect me to do. And so I got back on the train and went to school.

I like to think that I've put their good values to good use—I've been a social work administrator working with Native Americans for most of my adult life. In our home, whichever house it was, you respected people and you helped people without expecting anything in return. That's how a village works, and that's how I've tried to live my life.

—ROBERT CARR, Social worker
Hometown: Pueblo of Laguna Indian Reservation, New Mexico

The family sheep camp.

{Robert Castonguay, Jr.}

By the time I was six years old, I had lived in many houses but never really stayed long enough for any of them to feel like home. My father was in the navy, so we moved all along the Atlantic coast, from Texas to New Hampshire.

Then, in 1971, my mother and I moved to her parents' "summer place" in Seabrook Beach, New Hampshire. My father joined us a few months later.

It was a simple three-bedroom, one-story cottage. And I was home.

The first thing that made this house different (besides the fact that we stayed there!) was that its occupants spanned three wonderful generations. My parents and I lived there year-round, and my grandparents came to visit in the summer and on holidays. It was originally purchased as my grandparents' first vacation home, so—despite the fact that for my parents and me it was our only house—we always called it the Beach House.

The house was among the first of a group of houses built on a sandy peninsula that was part of the town of Seabrook. My grandfather John "Jack" Masterson purchased it in 1955 for a song. He was an accountant who worked for the Big Eight in the early twentieth century. The family had moved from town to town throughout the Northeast—from Long Island to Connecticut, on

The Beach House in Seabrook Beach, New Hampshire.

up to Massachusetts, and finally to New Hampshire—depending on where his clients were.

And then the company execs in the emerging Venezuelan oil industry wanted him down in Venezuela. This time, my grandfather balked. He went into business for himself, settling down with his wife and two daughters in Newburyport, Massachusetts. But I guess he missed New Hampshire. It was while he was living on the North Shore that he purchased the Beach House, where he would bring his family to vacation and relax. And where my mother would return with her husband and son to live.

When I think of the Beach House, I remember the wonderful parade of people who came through its front door; I remember the people more than the house itself. Perhaps that's because of the house's simple design: three bedrooms, a kitchen, porch, bathroom, and large living room with knotty pine paneling. To this day, whenever I enter a room that has knotty pine siding, it takes me back to my childhood home. The backyard was filled with beach sand. There was a vegetable garden. You could hear the waves and seagulls sounding off in the distance, and sunrise after sunrise set off summer days I wished would never end.

I loved getting to know my grandparents over the years and hearing their stories from a bygone era. Gramps was born in Indianapolis, Indiana, and loved to tell tales. He'd tell me all about Bat Masterson, the legendary character of the Old West who was everything from buffalo hunter and gambler to U.S. Army scout and sports editor—and who might, just might, have been a relative. He would tell me how he played catcher for the minor leagues in New Jersey and how he would have played for the Yankees if his knees hadn't given out. And he would tell me about New York City and the fifties—how one was the greatest city on earth and the other would never come again.

And Gramms would tell me about growing up as a farmer's daughter in New England. That was the secret to her long and healthy life, she said, and I believe her.

The Beach House was where it all happened for me. Elementary school and high school. My first real understanding of family. My first real lifelong friends. Every once in a while, I go back to what is now a bustling seaside town, home to a lot more vacation homes these days—not to mention a nuclear power plant.

I close my eyes, and it's summertime. The Fourth of July. People come to visit. We get together in the living room. Then it's off to the beach. We listen to the surf. It gets dark, and you can see the bonfires lining the beach from Seabrook to Salisbury.

The fireworks go off, and I am home.

—ROBERT CASTONGUAY, JR., Web site publisher
Hometown: Seabrook Beach, New Hampshire

ROBERT CASTONGUAY, JR.

{Eadie Churchill}

One of my earliest memories is a winter day in 1951. I am two years old, teetering on an auditorium seat beside my mother. I cry out, "Daddy!" as my father proceeds down the aisle. It is February, winter graduation for Miami University in Oxford, Ohio.

Any graduation is a proud occasion for the participants, but this particular commencement closed a very special chapter in the life of our young family. You see, my daddy's education was interrupted by World War II, an event that claimed his left leg, lodged shrapnel in his right, and forever altered his life. After the war, Daddy learned to cope with life as an amputee and married the woman who would soon be my Momma in 1946. First, my sister, Pam, arrived in 1947; I followed sixteen months later.

In 1949, my parents decided that a better future for our family depended on Daddy returning to school to complete his degree. Trouble was, there was still a postwar housing shortage, and a lot of veterans were going to school on the GI Bill. The combination made it hard to get on-campus housing and hard to afford off-campus housing. So we moved in with my maternal grandparents in Middletown, Ohio, and Daddy commuted the hour (twenty-two miles) to school while we waited for campus housing.

Finally, on January 2, 1950, we were able to move on campus into "Vet Village." Vet Village was made up of single- and double-wide trailers repurposed by the government to house student veterans and their families. The double-wide we were assigned had been a military office, so it had electricity, but it didn't have plumbing. Water came from the public bathhouse and laundry, where Daddy carried buckets to fill and then haul back to the trailer for cooking and toddler bathing, rain, snow, or shine.

Our one-room trailer was heated with a single "Heatrola" unit, and Momma cooked on a two-burner "white" gas stove. We had no refrigerator, but living on government disability compensation plus a small student allotment meant there was rarely very much that we needed to refrigerate. A bottom cabinet on an outside wall that stayed below freezing during the winter months was enough to keep our milk and butter. I asked Momma not too long ago how she felt about those living quarters—and it didn't surprise me when she replied enthusiastically that she would be thrilled to have the family together under one roof again.

Because I was so young, much of my memory of this house is from family stories, pictures,

My mother at the Vet Village—our bathhouse and laundry room
are in the background.

Our trailer at the Vet Village.

and visits back to Vet Village years after Daddy finished school. But I don't need first-hand memories to understand the importance of that period in our family's life.

The fourteen months we lived in that humble trailer and the example set by our parents has never left Pam or me. We have a deep love of learning, and we believe that true success comes from independence, perseverance, and making the most of every circumstance and opportunity.

When we were growing up, a favorite mealtime topic at our table was speculation about what Pam and I would do when we went off to college. Whether or not we would

My sister, Pam, and I playing in the snow around the Vet Village.

go wasn't a question—we were going. And sure enough, we both did—although life demonstrated its funny way of throwing surprises in our tracks, too. Our parents, of course, thought that our college careers would be easier than Daddy's, but war had something to say about that once again. This time it was the Vietnam War that was altering lives, and Pam and I both left school.

But the lessons of the trailer will never leave; like father like son, and like daughter, too. We left school, but we returned, and we finished. I went back after an eighteen-month hiatus, and Pam took a little longer but graduated cum laude—almost twenty years later!

As I said, Daddy's life was altered by losing his leg in the war. But Daddy was the kind of guy who was always going to make the most of his life with whatever he had to work with, never the kind of guy to give up. And he was the kind of guy who was always going to do the best he could for others with whatever he had. So after college, Daddy went to work for J. E. Hanger in Washington, D.C. He became a certified prosthetist. In 1958, he founded Faith Prosthetics in Concord, North Carolina, a small family business that has grown into a regional treatment center with six facilities across the Piedmont. Daddy died in 1995, but his legacy lives in all those he helped to walk again, to use an artificial limb and return to their lives, just as he had.

Some people think they're being served up lemons when life changes their plans. But Daddy and Momma always made the sweetest lemonade.

—EADIE CHURCHILL, Insurance executive
Hometown: Oxford, Ohio

{Kathryn Cline}

I don't come from what most people would consider a "broken" home, but it certainly wasn't conventional. I think sometimes things just come apart so that we can put them together ourselves. That's how our home was, starting with the way it was built. The house was sent in the form of a "kit" from Sears, Roebuck in the early part of the twentieth century to the Simons, a family who owned large tracts of land around Youngstown, Ohio. Because it could be conveniently delivered by train, the Simon family ordered a three-bedroom, one-bathroom ranch-style house and had it built on a one-acre lot in Boardman, a suburb of Youngstown. My parents then bought it years later, in 1947, for $9,000, succumbing to an increasingly common "white flight" out of more diverse areas like Youngstown.

Much like the house, our family also needed a little fitting together. My mother and father were still newlyweds when my father's former wife died and left four girls (ranging in age from seven to seventeen) to be looked after by my father and my mother, who was childless at the time. It wasn't until shortly after they moved to the house in Boardman that my parents had children together—my sister and then me. When I was still in a crib, I shared a bedroom with two other sisters. There was usually a line outside the only bathroom the eight of us shared. It was a tight squeeze, but the pieces of our family were held together by the small roof over our heads.

Because it huddled us close together, the house was always abuzz with sounds that I now miss. At night I fell asleep to my parents' low voices catching up on the day's news, and in the morning I awoke to the noise of a not-too-distant train whistle. I don't know why, but I looked forward to that train whistle, as if it were a greeting meant just for me.

On the other hand, being in that cramped space with a big family made me appreciate the outdoors. For a while we had a cornfield in our backyard where I used to ride my bicycle or play hide-and-seek between the rows. Later, we replanted the field with grass, and I would just lie there looking up at the sky, doing nothing but watching how fast the clouds moved. Those unstructured moments were the only flashes of peace and quiet. But I also loved helping Mother hang laundry back there. She would always fuss about the sheets hanging just so, and everything needing to be "white, white, white!" She was particular, much like the other moms in our homogeneous neighborhood. The Protestant values there ran deep and strong, right down to maintaining the gardens, keeping the homes tidy, and minding your own business.

Truth be told, life growing up was predictable. And I liked it that way. When family

Our Sears, Roebuck home in Youngstown, Ohio.

gathered (always in the dining room), I automatically knew where each member would sit before, during, and after dinner. It was always the same—the rhythm of speech, the stories, the jokes, the arguments, the compliments, the complaints. For me, home was the only place where people knew me and I knew them. There were no disguises, no pretenses, and all our expectations (both good and bad) were met.

My home was not nicely decorated or fancy, but we were proud and usually happy. How could this be when there were people so much better off financially than us? As I grew older, I realized that a house does not make a person. I learned our values did. Although most of my family was very conservative, we also recognized that we were all different. Those differences led to some healthy debates as well as some hard clashes. As the youngest, I watched some of my family members make good decisions and others make poor ones. I experienced how my own decisions allowed me to grow closer to some of them and caused me to grow more distant from others. But most important, I learned that I had the ability and the right to decide what kind of person I wanted to be. While my house informed my values, as an adult, my experiences helped to clarify what kind of person I chose to be. I, too, was made whole by piecing together my parts.

—KATHRYN CLINE, Health care worker
Hometown: Youngstown, Ohio

{Ben Cohen}

Justice and ice cream. If you get that, you get me. Throw half-gallon cardboard tubs, car rides through Harlem, and a Levittown ranch house in Merrick, Long Island, into the ice-cream maker of life, and out comes yours truly.

I was born in Brooklyn in 1951, but my parents moved to the house I grew up in, in Merrick, Long Island, before I was two. It was one of those mass-produced houses that William Levitt built across the Northeast as he helped to create the first American suburbs, seemingly overnight. A ranch house. Cedar shingles, brown on the outside, with a little front porch and a big picture window surrounded in red wood. There was fieldstone work around the house, a hedge in front of the porch, a big beautiful tree by the driveway, and a dogwood tree on the front lawn. The backyard of the 60' x 100' lot was filled with oaks, and there was this rickety fence all around the property that was made of skinny little logs and had a gate that was always falling off its hinges. I spent a lot of time "borrowing" my father's tools so I could fix that gate.

I was kind of a fat, nerdy kid, but I loved being outside. When I was eight or nine, my friends Lee and Fred and I spent an awful lot of time digging holes to China. Then, when I turned ten, I spent a few years struggling to grow vegetables on a little patch of ground in the backyard that I considered my private garden. I had about as much success with the garden as I did getting to China—until I turned to pumpkins, that is. Who knew that Merrick, Long Island, was pumpkin territory? As I got older, my attention turned—well, my attention was turned for me—to outside chores. A lotta years raking oak leaves, piling up oak leaves, jumping in piles of oak leaves, and burning piles of jumped-in oak leaves. This was right around the time most folks were making the big move from hand-pushed lawn mowers to powered mowers. My father didn't make the move—which meant a lotta years pushing mowers, too.

Yeah, my parents were big on chores. For some reason, my mother was all about cleaning my room, which was a real point of contention between us and led to a lot of strife. (Of course, years later, when I had to take up everything from plumbing, carpentry, and roof repair to keep our first ice-cream parlor in fighting trim, I suppose the early discipline of raking, mowing, and bed-making came in handy.)

I didn't have much fun in my bedroom—my mother put a Miro print over my bed, and I never really got into it. The truth is, I kind of resented it. That, and the Formica counter she installed as my desk. Which was for homework. Which must share an ancestor with chores. I could never get myself to do my homework, and my mother was always making me clear off the Formica counter, so that worked well, at least.

I loved our basement, probably because it was where we had the most fun. In the basement, we had a train set. And after the train set was gone, we had a Ping-Pong table. My father and I used to play on it, for money. Ten cents a game. Every night after dinner, my father would go downstairs to the basement—which he called the dungeon—where he had his little home office set up, and he would work on the work he took home with him. Accounting reports. And I was happy about it. Because behind the desk I had a workshop. I was interested in electricity. I liked making things. Hooking wires up to batteries and making lights light up and buzzers go buzz. I had some good times down there.

Upstairs, when you first came into the house, there was an L-shaped living room/dining room, where the family would all get together and watch sitcoms on TV. Looking every inch like a family in the fifties in a family sitcom about a family in the fifties. Beyond the living room was the kitchen. And that, you might say, turned out to be the most influential room in the house.

The whole family would have dinner at the kitchen table every night at 6:30. And one of the things that was pretty impressive about my father is that after dinner, before he went down to

Me, age four.

Our home in Merrick, New York.

the dungeon, he would take a half-gallon of ice cream out of the freezer and sit back down at the kitchen table with a soup spoon and consume a fair amount of that half-gallon. Sometimes you could watch him finish it. The flavor started out as Neapolitan—you know, that three-stripe mix of chocolate, vanilla, and strawberry. Then they started making a combination of chocolate and butter pecan, and he switched to that. But whatever flavor it was, the lesson was clear: Ice cream is *good*.

Yeah, well, what kid doesn't know that? I was a little more experimental than my father—I liked to *improve* my ice cream before I ate it. I always took my ice cream and put it into one of those little Pyrex cups and mixed, mashed, and stirred until it turned into soft ice cream. Then I'd break up pieces of candy and cookies and mix it in. If I'd known then what I know now, I'm sure I could have convinced my parents that I didn't need to do *all* that homework.

Sometimes my family would take trips in the car to New York City. And when we drove into New York City, we'd pass through Harlem. Now, when I was first growing up, not even an hour from Harlem, there was still a working farm on the corner near my house. When we drove through our neighborhood, we could name every family in every freshly painted house with its well-maintained lawn. Yet in Harlem, people were living in buildings that were falling apart, where there was garbage on the street and the windows were boarded up.

I would ask my father about it. Because I didn't like it. He would tell me that compared with other neighborhoods, there wasn't as much in the way of tax dollars coming out of Harlem, so the city didn't provide as much in the way of services. He said the sanitation department doesn't come as often; the police department doesn't come as often.

I didn't like that at all. I just didn't feel right about it. I knew it was wrong. I think those drives through Harlem ran right through me to kindle my sense of social justice and my commitment to fighting poverty.

Growing up in Merrick. Working hard (more or less) and having fun. And having the chance to see what the world was like outside Merrick. Harlem—and soon after, watching Martin Luther King and the whole civil rights movement unfold. Learning that people can make a difference.

That's the story of my life. Try to make people happy. Find a way to make a living and work to change a system that keeps people trapped in a cycle of poverty.

As Dr. King said, "True compassion is more than flinging a coin to a beggar; it comes to see that an edifice which produces beggars needs restructuring."

—BEN COHEN, Co-owner, Ben & Jerry's
Hometown: Merrick, New York

BEN COHEN

{ Benicio Del Toro }

In my home I learned to become who I am today. I came home to this house in Puerto Rico when I was born in 1967 and would not leave until 1981 when I went away to boarding school. With four, five, or six of us in the house at once, that's where I learned to be helpful, to respect my elders.

Our house is now seventy years old, still with the tiled floors in some rooms that had the most interesting geometric patterns. With high ceilings and thick walls, the place seemed bigger than it was. An almond tree out in the front curved around in the shape of a V. When my family bought the house, the owner asked us not to cut down the tree, which was planted in 1945, and the V represented Churchill's "V for Victory" campaign. That's where I learned how to be hopeful.

During the day there was the usual clamor of a neighborhood—radios playing, children shouting, church bells, the jingle of the ice cream vendor—but at night the air around was filled with the beautiful sound of the coquí, a small frog native to the island that sounds more like a bird. Dogs roamed through the backyard, which meant that it didn't always smell so good—but there was always a four-legged friend to play with.

We lived in the town of Santurce, a suburb of the capital, San Juan. Our neighborhood of Miramar is on several hills, and like its name suggests, it's not too far from the sea. The heart of our neighborhood is La Academia del Perpetuo Socorro, the local parochial school.

At home we spent most of our time gathered on the front porch, but I loved my room the most, if only because it was my own. Whenever I think of home, I think of my mother. She was such an influence on me. She taught me always to treat women with respect. She gave me a constant, unquenchable thirst for knowledge and understanding. And she inspired me to always enjoy life, every step.

I left my home in Puerto Rico over twenty years ago, but it remains with me still. I know that I will never forget where I came from. That's where I learned to be self-motivated, and that failure is never permanent. It's where I learned to dislike bullies—of any sort; to compete only with myself; and to never forget my friends. That's where I learned to be me.

—Benicio Del Toro, Actor
Hometown: Santurce, Puerto Rico

My sketch of my house in Puerto Rico.

BENICIO DEL TORO

{Bob Dole}

I began life in a modest wooden dwelling

close to the Union Pacific tracks that reminded residents of Russell, Kansas, several times a day of a world beyond the wheat fields and oil rigs of Russell County. I suspect that the loudest of train whistles was drowned out by the sounds of four people—my parents, my infant sister, Gloria, and me—who shared three rooms, including a lean-to kitchen. I say "suspect" because I was too young to remember much about the place. When my brother Kenny was born a year after me, we moved into a bigger house on the corner of Eleventh and Maple. It had five rooms instead of three. In time, there were four Dole children sharing one room, a bike, and a pair of roller skates.

I long ago outgrew my boyhood house. But I have never outgrown my boyhood home, and hope I never will. A house, after all, is a roof over your head. A home is a classroom of character, usually a classroom without walls. In this case, home was a small town whose sense of community was as vast as the Kansas prairie. Few of my neighbors had much in material terms. Even before the so-called Dirty Thirties, when the Dust Bowl enveloped Kansas and topsoil blew away in the parched conditions of near permanent drought, we didn't dwell on what we didn't have. Rather, we enjoyed high school track meets and Fourth of July firecrackers and homemade butter and *The Owl Show*, a late night performance at the Dream Theater. If your school attendance record measured up, there were free passes to the Hoot Gibson matinee on Saturday afternoon.

Our home was blessed with values that couldn't—and can't—be measured in dollars and cents. Home included my dad's creamery station on Main Street, where he cracked jokes and established a reputation for fair dealing when purchasing milk, eggs, or the big cans of sour cream I helped him load onto eastbound cars of the Union Pacific. Like many Kansans, Dad was laconic by nature. If you mowed the lawn to perfection, you treasured his "pretty good" all the more because compliments were rarer than seagulls in west-central Kansas. My father divided the world into two groups of people, doers and stewers. He belonged to the former camp.

So did my mother. In our house, cleanliness gave godliness a run for its money. Mom saw to that. As kids, we sat on dining room chairs, hitching up our legs so they wouldn't touch the floor that Mom had just washed and waxed. Waiting for that floor to dry was a lesson in patience. Not to mention the kind of self-control that would serve me well during Senate filibusters. A true homemaker, Mom adored Christmas. When not demonstrating the exact way to drape a tree in tinsel, she taught us the true meaning of the season. Presents of the store-bought variety were rare, but spiritual gifts were plentiful.

When it came to clothes, we were among the richest of Russellites—at least as long as Mom's sewing machine held out. Given the economic realities of the time, she worked outside the home long before it became fashionable. Day after day, she would leave the house lugging a bulky sewing machine or vacuum cleaner whose virtues she demonstrated for prospective customers. She might still be gone when we arrived home from school in the afternoon to find baked treats she had left out for us. Her magic touch extended to the kitchen as well as the sewing machine. Many's the time I heard her say, "Can't never could do anything." Is it any wonder, during the difficult post–World War II years of recuperation and renewal, that my thoughts often went back to the small frame house on Maple Street?

Thanks to my dad's sly wit, there was no shortage of laughter inside its walls. That, too, formed a big part of my education. I was nine years old when we moved again, to a place just down the street. Long before then, I had learned that laughter is not only the best medicine—it's also the best antidote to what, in a later life, I would recognize as Potomac fever. However crowded it might be, the one thing for which that house—that home—had no room was self-importance.

—BOB DOLE, Former U.S. Senator
Hometown: Russell, Kansas

Our home in Russell, Kansas.

{Gary Eisner}

I grew up in a public housing project in Cleveland in the late forties and fifties. It was the Lee-Seville housing projects in the southeast part of town. They were built after World War II and torn down in the sixties, but they were the first and most important home I knew. I lived there from 1946, the year I was born, until 1957. There were four of us, my father, mother, brother, and me, in a one-level, two-bedroom home.

The house had one very small bathroom with a shower and no tub, a small kitchen with a utility room to the side, and a small living room with a coal-burning stove. In front of the house was a very small yard that had a coal bin off to the side. The back of the house bordered on a vast field. The floors were all linoleum and smelled damp all the time. The linoleum was ugly, old, and dingy. The smell of coal from the bin permeated the house, but in the spring and summer, the wildflowers growing in the field filled the air with prettier fragrances, so sweet smells competed with dank ones for our attention.

Cleveland in the forties and fifties was a factory town with an industry-driven economy. Steel companies like Republic Steel and Jones & Laughlin were the big employers. Most of the city's residents were blue-collar and came from every corner of the world. We had the largest Hungarian population outside of Hungary, and neighborhoods included Little Italy and Chinatown.

The Lee-Seville neighborhood was entirely African American except for my family and two other families. It was a time of great racial prejudice in America, but I did not know this. I was too young to know about Emmett Till or Rosa Parks. The only friends I had were African Americans.

The truth is, the other two white families hated me and my family because we were Jewish. I will never forget the day that the father of one of the white families passed peaches out to all the kids standing in front of his yard except me. The father looked at me and said, "Why don't you go home, you Jew?"

Or the day that the oldest daughter of the other white family bought ice cream for all the kids who were playing baseball in front of her yard. I stood last in line behind the Good Humor ice cream truck, waiting for my treat, only to be told that the oldest daughter of one family wouldn't buy ice cream for me because I was Jewish.

I was seven years old. I didn't understand.

Living in that house off Telfair Avenue in the Lee-Seville projects was the single most influential life experience I have had, even though forty-seven years have passed since I have left. I worked my way through college; I worked my way through law school. I've been a practicing lawyer for thirty-two years. But nothing could have prepared me better for the realities of life than experiencing life as a minority in a minority.

I learned that prejudice can only be learned. When white and black children grow up together, play together, go to school together, and share their lives together, hatred and fear of each other is alien to them. They accept each other because of what they have in common and haven't been taught to fear what is different.

Most of my childhood unfolded in the company of acceptance and understanding, punctuated rarely by the sharp touch of prejudice. In the projects, so long ago, I learned what I want in my life and what I don't. The only thing that really deserves intolerance is intolerance itself.

Five years ago, I was appointed by the Cuyahoga County Common Pleas Court to represent a young African American accused of drug trafficking. I knew that my client's father disliked me from the moment he met me. Finally, the father said to me, "How can a rich Jewish lawyer like you ever know what it's like to grow up and live on Tarkington Avenue?"

I just smiled and said, "Because I grew up one street over on Telfair Avenue in the Lee-Seville projects."

—GARY EISNER, Lawyer
Hometown: Cleveland, Ohio

The view from the Lee-Seville housing projects in Cleveland, Ohio.

Imagine coming of age in the middle of an industrial town in the middle of the country in the middle of the century, snuggled against the muddy banks of the Mississippi River during World War II. We lived in a closely packed neighborhood, struggling to understand the larger world and make ends meet in the shadow of the courthouse, while the United States struggled to come of age in the shadow of the atomic bomb.

In Clinton, Iowa, there were no televisions, no professional sports, no big automobiles or manicured lawns, but we had radios, movies, high school sports, and the Clinton Industrial Summer Baseball League. We had victory gardens, drove old jalopies, took the bus, or rode bicycles. The Clinton County Courthouse cast a shadow across our neighborhood of two-parent homes and stay-at-home moms, and the four faces of its magnificent clock chimed every half hour. Most of our parents had no education beyond grammar school, and nearly all of our fathers worked at the factories or on the railroad.

In the hot weather, families slept with windows open, doors unlocked, and bicycles against the side of the house, knowing neither neighbor nor stranger would disturb their possessions. In winter, schools never closed, even when snowbanks mounted four feet high on both sides of the walks. This was my world against the backdrop of the courthouse—St. Patrick's Elementary School, Riverview Stadium, Clinton downtown, and Mill Creek. We kids ran around entertaining ourselves, as our parents were often too tired, too involved in the war effort, or too busy making a living to pay us much mind.

In the shadow of the courthouse there was a grocer, Frank Cramm; a family physician, Dr. Joseph O'Donnell; an eyes, ears, nose, and throat specialist, Dr. Ed Carey; a family dentist, Dr. John McLaughlin; a family barber, Robert "Ripper" Collins; family tavern keepers, Harvey Sullivan and Leon Cavanaugh; and even a family mortician, Johnny Dalton.

My da (Irish for dad) was never more at home than in the company of fellow Irishmen. At our place, the coffeepot was always perking on the gas burner. You could usually find my mother at the kitchen table singing to herself as she whipped up a chocolate fudge cake in preparation for the arrival of the clan. On Wednesdays, the group included my da's co-worker at the railroad Bill Knight, my uncle Bill Clegg, saloon keeper Leo Sullivan and his wife, Alice, my mother's girlfriend Cleo Hyde, and my mother's brothers and their wives.

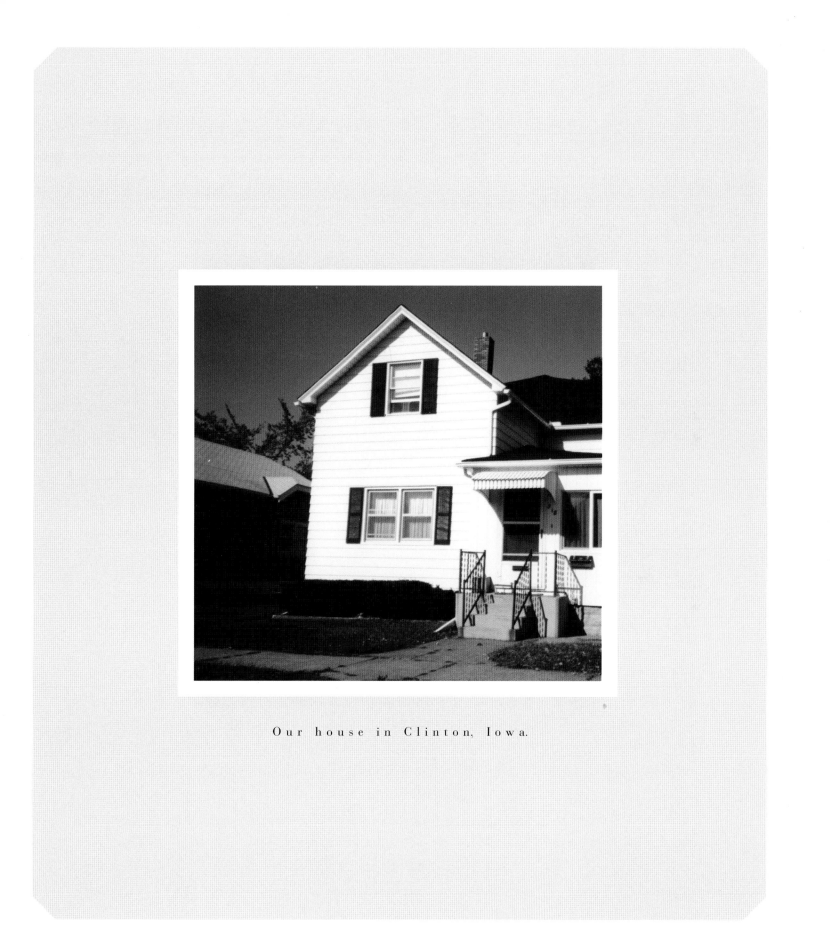

Our house in Clinton, Iowa.

JAMES FISHER

The Clinton County courthouse.

I would peek down the stairs to listen to their conversation, even though I was supposed to be in bed. When the storytelling began, my ears would perk up. My da was a listener, while my mother (who was hard of hearing) would busy herself cleaning the ashtrays and refilling coffee cups. Uncle Bill would clear his throat, and the room would grow quiet. Methodically, he would pack his pipe, light it, take a slow, deliberate drag on it, and then launch theatrically into his latest story, invariably related to his misgivings about the war effort. His thoughtful confidence mesmerized me, as did his crusty voice and a gaze that seemed to look over everyone's head as if he were seeing beyond them. No one ever interrupted Uncle Bill (even though to say something against President Roosevelt in my house was a sacrilege) out of respect for his son, Jack, a U.S. sailor who was almost killed at Pearl Harbor.

The house itself was a one-and-one-half-story white clapboard box with a green-shingled pitched roof that we bought for $3,000. My da borrowed the $300 down payment from my Uncle Arne. My mother told me he was never able to repay it, but bachelor Uncle Arne didn't mind—he received suitable compensation in coffee, chocolate cake, shared cigarettes, and a place to go every night after work.

The house was small, a little over a thousand square feet, but still divided into four bedrooms, a formal dining room, kitchen, bathroom, and full basement. The basement had a terribly low ceiling, and even at eight, already 4'11', I could not stretch to my full height. It was damp and always cold, even in the summer. There was a small bedroom on the first floor that adjoined the stairwell. For us, it was the radio room, occupied by a reading lamp, a large padded sofa, a love seat, and a small credenza. My mother would read to us out of books checked out from the public library, or we would sit around the radio and listen to the high jinx of Amos 'n' Andy, Fibber McGee and Molly, Fred Allen's program *Allen's Alley*, or, more seriously, to the "fireside chats" of President Roosevelt.

The master bedroom was off limits to us kids, but the glass door covered in lace curtains taunted us. I managed to sneak in a few times to find ashtrays everywhere: on both sides of the bed, on the dresser, and on a chair. What made the room special, however, were ceramic frescoes of Jesus and the Blessed Virgin Mother that my parents brought from Chicago.

Leo Cavanaugh, who owned the Silver Rail Saloon, repapered the walls of the living and dining rooms, in patterns that didn't always mesh. It was as if he created a wall montage, and I loved it. My favorite spot was the dining room table, a large, mahogany beauty that nearly filled the entire room. Its four chairs were jammed into the room's four corners, along with a mahogany bureau stuffed against the back wall. Here I would draw and write my little stories, imagining myself the hero of whatever tale I spun. When I tired of this, I would study the dictionary and try my new words on my mother in often inappropriately constructed sentences with something approaching religious zeal. "Language is the tool of the mind," she would often say, "and since you must think with words, you must master them if you are to think clearly."

Our courthouse neighborhood house was our first real home. For the first eight years of my life, we moved constantly from one rental place to another, always having to leave because my da couldn't come up with the rent. Once we were in our new home, my mother said, "Go and explore the house, then write it down, and I'll read it, and grade you on it." With her, school was never out, but she probably also wanted me out of her hair. Besides, exploring was part of my nature. I paced off the distance from the house next door to the property line on the other side in three-foot steps: sixty-four feet. Then I walked from the front curb to the back of our property: one hundred and ten feet. The house, I found, was forty feet wide, and thirty feet long. I took out my pencil and wrote it down in my little notebook.

Next I surveyed the property. A delicious apple tree sat outside the dining room window, and currant berry bushes, a small asparagus patch, and a crab apple tree were all just behind the house. A crumbling cement walk divided the backyard symmetrically, with intertwined vines on the edges and ending at a three-tiered chicken coop to the west of the walk and a small garage to the east (but we had no automobile). A plum tree was directly in front of the chicken coop and a pear tree in front of the garage, creating a kind of orchard. The chicken coop fascinated me, and I envisioned it as my secret place, which it soon became. I kept my comic books there and put pictures of my heroes on the walls. I even made a small altar to the Blessed Virgin Mary. It took a lot of work to clean up, but I knew it would be "my place" and no one else's.

Now, more than seventy years after the house was first built, it stands proudly and defiantly against time, but without the chicken coop, the garage, the grapevines, the fruit trees, or the garden. Luckily, I took all the important things with me in my mind. I took to heart my mother's words at that dining room table and trained my imagination in that chicken coop. I may not remain in that house anymore, but that house remains in me.

—JAMES FISHER, Retired corporate executive
Hometown: Clinton, Iowa

{Marcia Fountain-Blacklidge}

As I sit down to describe the house where I grew up, it's hard to reconcile the profusion of memories and feelings that wash over me with the reality of a 1,200-square-foot box divided into three bedrooms, a kitchen, living room, bath, and utility room. How could such a small space have produced the extraordinary warmth that embraced me when I came in from the cold? How could our tiny living room have accommodated a sofa large enough for everyone to snuggle into? How could our kitchen possibly fit a table that always had room for family and friends to share a meal and so much more? At a glance, our house didn't look like a dream home, but we all know looks can be deceiving. In many ways, the house my parents built in 1953 was perfect, and, hopefully, still is.

My mother, father, older sister, and I moved into our home in Griffith, Indiana, when I was four years old. My younger brother and sister would be born while we were there. We moved to the town when it was growing and optimistic. Our neighborhood was mostly comprised of young, working-class families. Most of the fathers on our block worked in the steel mills while the mothers stayed home. My father was one of the few men who had a college degree.

Lining the back of our neighborhood were cornfields and woods we used to explore without fear. From kindergarten until junior high school, I walked more than a mile to school, always feeling safe and secure.

Things began to change the day President Kennedy was assassinated. At first our school was abuzz with rumors that something terrible had happened. Then our principal came on the loud-speaker and announced that the president had been shot. When he dismissed school, an eerie silence filled the hallways as we shuffled to our lockers.

The world came to a stop. Everyone I knew was glued to the television trying to stay connected to the rest of the nation. The Sunday morning that I watched Lee Harvey Oswald get shot to death on live television, I promptly threw up on our living room carpet. A new, more frightening world had, without warning, moved in and evicted my innocence.

As many people do when things are changing, I craved information. So I became a fervent reader—and then I began to crave privacy, but that was hard to come by when a family of six occupies only 1,200 square feet. I found mine in the closet at the end of our hall and it became my retreat. A garment rod hanging end to end filled one side of the closet with out-of-season clothes and coats while a ceiling-high row of boxes was crammed into the other. Beneath the

My childhood home in Griffith, Indiana.

garments was just enough room for me to make a nest, and I would read there for hours by flashlight. Once a week, I'd walk to the library where the librarian, concerned about the number of books I could safely carry, wisely limited me to the number that would comfortably fit between my elbow and shoulder.

One day, I chose a book for no other reason than it was thin, which meant I could check out five books instead of my usual four. I decided to read the lightest book first, but I would soon discover it was heavier than any book I'd ever read.

My father spent many years in what he called an "orphanage." He was a Native American, and when he was young, he didn't know that the school he called an "orphanage" was one of many forced boarding schools created by the United States government in the late 1800s to deal with the "Indian problem." Generations of Indian children were removed from their homes and placed in boarding schools in an attempt to eradicate their culture and assimilate them into "white society."

My father didn't like to talk about his experience in the orphanage—it was a place he didn't want to revisit, even in his mind—but he had shared those memories with my mother and I asked her about them. She told me the authorities were cruel, and that my father often went to bed hungry. When he was seven, my father broke his leg badly, but he was forced to lie in pain until they finally allowed him an operation. When he healed, he decided he had to escape. My father did, but he found that his entire family had moved away; luckily, some neighbors took him in.

As you can imagine, ripping a child away from his family and heritage is traumatic and devastating. Although the government certainly wasn't trying to eliminate these children, it was eliminating their cultural and family connections, and for that reason it has sometimes been compared to the Holocaust.

The thin book I borrowed from the library was the story of an Auschwitz survivor. When I finished, I was amazed to discover I felt better. I didn't understand why; I just knew I had to read more. And I did. Each experience taught me something and also freed me from something. My mom explained that the way dad grew up left many lessons unlearned, like how important it is to hug the people you love, how to set reasonable rules, and how to trust others. He was always a strict disciplinarian, and sometimes it was hard to understand why. Dinner at 6:00, no talking at the table, eat everything on your plate, no questions asked. At last, I was learning why. Finally, after many books, I came to the point where I'd cried through the pain I felt for my father, and now I could see him more clearly. He never really had a home, but he soared above the suffering of his childhood and built one for us.

After everything he went through, he met and married the woman of his dreams, got an engineering degree from Michigan State, built a home, and raised a loving family. He never submitted to the life sentence that "orphanage" tried to hand him, but, instead, worked even harder to gain education, self-worth, and compassion. His resilience ended up being so much stronger than the pain he carried, and I will never forget this proof that we can beat anything. I never went back to the closet after that summer. I couldn't. I'd outgrown it—from the inside out.

What I learned in that closet at the end of the hall was underscored years later, after we'd all left home. When my mother passed away (my father had already left us), my siblings and I all gathered in Michigan for her burial. Because we were all going our separate ways, we said our good-byes at the cemetery. Around dinnertime, I spotted a sign for a restaurant that had been a favorite of my family's when I was a child, and we decided to stop. As we sat there, each of my siblings wandered one by one into the restaurant. Sharing a meal together soothed our hearts and created a beginning for us as the elder generation of our family. When we departed, the rain that had fallen all day gave way to a beautiful double rainbow that filled the sky. I like to think that was our parents watching over us, reminding us to trust the power of our family's love—because you can't hide in a closet forever.

—MARCIA FOUNTAIN-BLACKLIDGE, Writer
Hometown: Griffith, Indiana

{Tommy Franks}

"Ain't this a great country?" Those words fill my head as I think about the house where I was raised. I was born in 1945 in Wynnewood, Oklahoma, a small but prosperous farming community—home to an oil refinery and lots of petro-service businesses. Adopted at birth, I went home with the only parents I've ever known—Ray and Lorene Franks. My father, just returned from service in World War II, was a banker and a farmer; he was also an ardent supporter of the Wynnewood High School Savages—one of the best small school football teams in Oklahoma. My mother was a homemaker and loving mother. Just as they were the only parents I've ever known, I was the only child they would ever have.

We lived in a small farmhouse at the edge of town. It was both lovely and unusual because our farm—a few hundred acres—was behind the house, but we had neighbors on both sides, which gave the place a "city look." Quite a special place for a kid—playmates up and down the street and a farm with animals, barns, and rich black dirt where I "worked" as a kid with my dad.

My earliest memories include the smiles of loving parents, smells in the kitchen where my mother cooked and the family ate, wooden floors that creaked, and the TV in the living room. What a prize. This must have been 1948 or 1949, and I'm sure we were among the first in town to own a TV.

I treasure memories of tractor rides with my dad, the family sitting on the front porch, the smell of rain, watching my parents hold hands…and the security of that old house.

It was in that two-bedroom farmhouse that I got my earliest lessons on the value of unconditional love, the importance of being with family, and how it feels to "be at peace." With maturity came increased understanding of responsibility, integrity, ambition, freedom…and its cost.

I served in the military for almost four decades…and I can't count the times I was drawn back to my youth for the answer to a problem or dilemma. There is certain strength in understanding where you come from and what it means to have a "home place." There is certain pride in remembering my dad's service to our country and his hard work to give me the chance to build a bright future. And there is certain comfort in remembering my mother's love, cooking in the kitchen, entertaining in our living room.

My roots run deep, deep in the black dirt that sits under an old house in Oklahoma.

—TOMMY FRANKS, Former U.S. General
Hometown: Wynnewood, Oklahoma

My childhood home in Wynnewood, Oklahoma.

{Richard M. Frias}

Above me is the pitter patter on the plaster
ceiling. To my left and to my right is the loud music of the inner city converted into tranquil sounds as it passes through the walls I have come to know so well. Below me, the ramblings of a family as they hear what I hear, in the never-ending cycle of apartment life. This is where I live. The Bronx. Growing up here is growing up in a shared universe, never alone and never quiet, engulfed by the scent, sound, and sight of others.

I remember the first time I moved into my apartment. To my young eyes the huge complex was a maze invented for the sole purpose of "hide and seek" or "cops and robbers." Just a few blocks away lay the pinnacle of New York pride—Yankee Stadium. Yankee Stadium is the one place where the inner city and its outer precincts become one as everyone comes together to cheer for the home team. The first time I ever saw a Yankee game I thought that the entire world had come to The Bronx. Riding the subway home after a game was always a cheerful event fueled by the victory cries of faithful fans.

I understand now that the comfort and power of an apartment building isn't just found in the promise of shelter or the hope (not always realized) of hot water. When your home is an apartment building, everyone knows your name, business, dreams, and flaws without ever speaking to you. And you learn that the walls don't hold secrets as well as you'd like to think.

I remember watching the women, who spoke of all and feared nothing, as they sat outside the building. I remember watching the men, who stood across the street from the women, as they had passionate debates about baseball and boxing. Most important, I remember watching the children, scattered around the sidewalks, as they tried to imitate the men and women. I didn't witness the violence portrayed on television; I witnessed a community created by the block's youth and elderly.

The memory of being a seven-year-old waiting for my father to come home from work will never leave me. The steel door became my partner as I counted the minutes until my father would complete our family circle and my mother would cook the best food in the Bronx. As I reflect on it now, I realize that the overwhelming feeling I had when I watched my parents rest their aching bodies and weary souls was pride. Pride in their work ethic—pride in the family they built. In our apartment, ideas were encouraged and when they were expressed, they were nurtured. Inside those walls we bared our souls and let each other know the pain and the happiness that only life can create. No dream was ever out of reach and no hope was ever too high.

On paper, I am an only child but in The Bronx my brothers and sisters were the neighbors below, above, and around me. When one neighbor left, a little piece of my apartment was taken away and the memories, later fading into the dreams of a man, were all that remained. I often think of the times when my mother and I would sit on the fire escape listening and watching our shared universe. Our neighbors would either bring us something to eat or ignore us—either way, we didn't need to speak, we didn't need any other communication.

And then there was stickball. It was only during stickball games that the men across the street would join the women sitting by the building and the scattered children would remain still. I have always believed that our concrete field is a perfect example of urban ingenuity. First base was the right side of the fire hydrant, second base was the middle of the street, third base was the car in front of the lamp post, and home was wherever you batted from. The type of ball used would set the mood of the game. If it was a rubber ball, chaos was coming. If it was a tennis ball, the losing team would complain. And if it was a baseball, all bets were off and every person on the concrete field would take the game seriously. Along the sidelines, old men would always give the pitcher advice—here's how to throw the perfect curve ball; here's how to psyche this batter out. The game ended when nine innings were over or when every mother would yell from the top of her lungs, whichever came first. On summer nights the games would last until sundown and everyone was happy to be alive.

Home is where the heart of your loved ones can be found and the pride in your heritage first grows. I do not envy those who live in the suburbs. The flaws in our community and our building were accepted; they were loved. My stars are my streetlights, my sound of the ocean is the music played by the fire hydrant on a hot summer day. My block is my home...my home is my block. My home is The Bronx.

—Richard M. Frias, Student
Hometown: The Bronx, New York

The view from my apartment window.

{John Glenn}

I grew up in the same home from infancy until I left for military flight training after Pearl Harbor.

New Concord, Ohio (POPULATION 1185, read the sign at the east end of Main Street in those days), was the home of Muskingum College, which added a thousand students to the population when college was in session. Our home was located along old Route 40, the first truly national road that went from coast to coast. In earlier days, the road had started as the Zane Trace Trail, followed by settlers, wagons, and stagecoaches westward bound. In fact, the Great Plains actually start about thirty miles to the west.

I am admittedly prejudiced, but I believe that small-town Midwest America is an ideal childhood environment, and home was the center. That's where young people were shaped. That's where their values were formed. That's where their hopes and dreams were talked about, encouraged, and planned. That's where their heartfelt loyalties to God and country were nurtured and supported by the whole community.

I have been exceptionally fortunate in later years to see that house—my home—preserved, restored, and refurnished to exactly the way it was when I was a boy. The home is now the John and Annie Glenn Historic Site, with a fully equipped classroom and teaching area for presentations to school groups and other visitors.

The focal point, however, is the restored and refinished home itself. For me, it's like a return to boyhood when I step through the front door. For visitors, it's made more real by the college faculty and student volunteers who in period dress act the part of my mother while conducting tours as though it is "back when"—the days of my childhood. And "back when" includes such experiences as the Great Depression, which remains vivid to me to this day.

In fact, one of the most memorable conversations I recall from that period was overhearing my dad and mother after dinner one evening, still sitting at the table, talking quietly about the probability that the mortgage was going to be foreclosed on our house—our home—and what we would do, where we would go, who we would or could live with. I assure you, that conversation struck terror into the heart of a ten-year-old. Shortly thereafter, President Roosevelt's New Deal became law; the Federal Housing Administration was formed to provide insurance for home loans, the Works Progress Administration provided work, our loan was extended, and our home

My home in New Concord, Ohio.

was saved. That event undoubtedly affects me to this day, in my attitude about the government's proper role in times of emergency.

I also remember what it was like in World War II with full mobilization, service star flags in the windows, and rationing stamps. "Oh, yes, here are some of them here on the sink that I haven't used yet," my volunteer "mother" says, acting out a part as though they are in World War II, and the children get to see actual ration stamps from those days. And how we saved tinfoil and grease fat drippings, and what it was like with an icebox refrigerator, and on and on. Across the country, families were serving America in small ways and large, and I imagine that helped set me on a course that would see me serving my country all the way to the moon. (And then back to Washington, which might be an even stranger place.)

I'm very glad that the home I remember so well still stands and is being used again to motivate our young people.

If, after all these years, it can foster in the children of today a sense of values, of wonder and curiosity, encourage in even a small way their hopes and dreams, and maybe even advance their own feelings and loyalties to God and country, then it is still serving a noble and necessary purpose, as a good home should, as my good home did for me.

—JOHN GLENN, Former astronaut and U.S. Senator
   Hometown: New Concord, Ohio

{Danny Glover}

The first house my family owned was in the

Haight-Ashbury section of San Francisco. We moved into it in 1957, when I was eleven years old. Before that, we lived in subsidized housing. We were among a group of families first to move into a mixed neighborhood, away from the two neighborhoods in San Francisco that had been home to African Americans.

Our neighborhood was made up of newer houses adjacent to Golden Gate Park, built in the twenties like ours, and older ones—big houses—some had been owned by shipping magnates.

We lived upstairs and rented out the downstairs. I can tell you what our house looked like, but the thing I remember most is what living in it was like. The thing about my home was that everyone participated in the work that had to be done. When we had to paint the house, my dad, my brother Reginald, and I painted the house. When cleaning needed to be done, someone would mop the kitchen floor, someone would wax the kitchen floor, someone would clean the bathroom.

If we were cooking Saturday night dinner, one of us had to be peeling potatoes, one of us had to be frying potatoes. I learned how to cook because that was a responsibility we all shared. All the boys knew how to cook. My dad knew how to cook.

There are twelve years between my youngest brother, Martin, and me—so you know what that meant. I had to babysit Martin; I had to change him; I had to bathe him. So did the other children who were old enough. All those things we did, we all had to do. A lot of that structure was the structure my mom had when she was growing up on a cotton farm in Georgia. Everyone worked on the farm, everyone picked cotton, everyone had a responsibility.

And you combine that with the pride, the sense of ownership, the whole idea of middle-class aspiration—well, you can see why it was so important to us. Still is today. Because we all knew that when we had to clean out the junk in the basement—it was our junk and our basement, you know?

All of my siblings have owned homes. It's no surprise. I think that's how family works; I think that's a little bit of what home is. Conscientiousness goes from one generation to the next; the values of your parents that become yours in the watching and the doing.

For us, it was equanimity and responsibility, ownership and aspiration. And the idea that you work together, that the family becomes an organization where everybody puts their own personal agenda aside to contribute to the agenda of the whole. Mutual support and collaboration and teamwork—this was a very poignant part of what I felt growing up.

Of course, there was also lots of fun to be had. The neighborhood was exciting, changing, moving all the time. A big multigenerational family lived across the street. I think they may have been from Arkansas, but what I really remember was people—grandparents, cousins, aunts, and uncles—filling three floors. Seven boys and two or three girls. I still have dreams about that house. You could make up a baseball or basketball team with them. Go to Golden Gate Park. Play football. And always make up a reason to fight afterward.

There was music on those streets. Leon Pattilo lived right down the block. He had a band, played piano with those long hands he had, sang lead vocals with Santana. His father was a cab driver. You could always find musicians hanging out at their house, and music coming out of it. Sly Stone was a DJ then, and he used to come sit in all the time. Three doors down was Bobby Freeman, who had a red Impala and a big hit with "Do You Wanna Dance?"

We used to stand on the corner and I would sing like Smokey Robinson. And then we'd run off to the park, up to the high school for basketball, or just play football in the streets and make believe we were Joe "The Jet" Perry or Alan Ameche or "Alley Oop" Owens.

And then it was home. You'd come up the steps into the living room, with the kitchen next to it and one tiny bathroom for all seven of us. Next was the dining room and then the hallway leading to the bedrooms, with a large, tall heater, heating the whole house. Back to the left was my parents' room, to the right was the room my sister and my youngest brother shared. You'd have to go through their room to get to what would have been the sun porch—but instead was the older boys' room, three of us in there, me and my two other brothers. That was my room, but it wasn't my own place, and with all that activity, inside and out, sometimes you just needed a place of your own, you know?

The room I cared about most wasn't a room at all; it was the space between the dining room and the bedrooms. I always found myself getting up in the middle of the night just to stretch out in front of the heater and create a space for myself. My mother used to wake up for work and find me there. In between washing dishes, I would lay there. In between doing homework—when I did my homework—I would lay there. It was my sleeping space and my day-dreaming space— you know, where you'd dream about the girl you liked who hasn't said two words to you in the two months since you've been liking her.

It was just my space. That's what home is, after all. A place to call your own, to take care of, to grow in, in the company of the people and the things you love.

—DANNY GLOVER, Actor
Hometown: San Francisco, California

Our house in
San Francisco,
California.

{Franklin Graham}

Home has always been a refuge, an escape, and a haven from the pressures and demands of life.

The only home that my wife, Jane, and I have ever owned is a small five-bedroom, two-and-a-half-bath farmhouse built in the late 1860s. It sits on an old mountain farm just off the Blue Ridge Parkway between Boone and Blowing Rock, North Carolina. Mowing pastures and fixing fences aren't a chore, but a pleasant break from the hectic pace of leading two large evangelistic ministries.

I have always lived in western North Carolina. My parents' home just outside of Montreat is a log home with five fireplaces. Some of my fondest memories are of sitting around the fire in the kitchen, where my father would lead our family in devotions every morning and evening. Even to this day, there might be two or three fires in different rooms, breaking the mountain chill. When I think of home, whether it's my parents' house or the home where Jane and I live today, it is always a place of love and family.

The Bible has a lot to say about the home. No matter where my lot in life is here on this earth, the Scriptures tell me that, as a follower of Jesus Christ, I have an eternal home. Jesus told

My family outside our home in
Montreat, North Carolina.

Our current home in western North Carolina.

His disciples as He prepared to die on the cross for our sins: "Let not your heart be troubled; ye believe in God, believe also in Me. In My Father's house are many mansions; if it were not so, I would have told you. I go to prepare a place for you and if I go to prepare a place for you, I will come again, and receive you unto Myself, that where I am, there ye may be also" (John 14:1–3).

The earthly home where Jane and I have lived for almost thirty years and raised our four children will one day be gone. So will we all, but I know that I have a heavenly home. It's not because of any good that I may have done, but simply because of what Christ did for all of us on the cross two thousand years ago.

When I was twenty-two years old, I received Jesus Christ into my heart by faith, and my life has never been the same. When this life is over, I'll be in my final home—heaven—a place built not by human hands, but by God Himself.

I believe this same wonderful hope can be yours, too, simply by trusting in Jesus Christ as I did and receiving Him as Lord and Savior. I thank God for a peaceful, lovely home on earth, but I am even more thankful for my heavenly home that will last for eternity.

—FRANKLIN GRAHAM, President and CEO, Billy Graham Evangelical Association
Hometown: Montreat, North Carolina

FRANKLIN GRAHAM

{Nanci Griffith}

When I was old enough to ride my bike around town, I would leave my house in south Austin, stop at my grandparents' house in central Austin, and branch off to visit friends in north Austin. My grandparents' house was the hub—no matter where I was coming from or where I was going to, I passed through it.

That's how it always was. My parents were beatniks; I spent more time at my grandparents' house than with either of my parents. It was the center of my life.

My grandparents were the children of Welsh immigrants. They originally lived in a house downtown on the riverbank, but a great flood destroyed much of downtown in 1935. So they decided to get away from the river—and they built their new house in what was then the outskirts of town but is now central Austin.

It was a great big house, filled with rooms just made for wandering, each bearing the distinctive stamp of one of my grandparents or blending their styles in unexpected but beautiful harmony. Their bedrooms were probably the purest expression of their individual styles. My grandmother had heart trouble, and my grandfather snored. It might not seem that those two conditions were related, but they were afraid my grandfather's snoring would startle her awake and her heart would give out from fright! So they had separate bedrooms. Hers was delicate, all lace and little porcelain boxes. His was leather, crisp, and military straight.

Their styles were a reflection of their personalities. My grandmother was a wonderful spirit, full of love and childlike excitement. She was always the first one to the tree on Christmas morning, and she'd shake every present with her name on it until it was broken. She loved to collect things—she had a beautiful collection of porcelain boxes and ashtrays that my uncle brought her from Japan after his service in World War II. And like most grandmothers who lived through the Depression, she had an enormous collection of buttons. She loved it all.

My grandfather *seemed* different—he put out a tough, gruff exterior to the world, and all the children were afraid of him. But I knew it was all a big facade. I must have been around eight when he wanted to teach me about money. So we would set up a little store in the garage, with a cigar box for a cash register and some of my grandmother's buttons for money. She also collected soup cans and cereal boxes and milk bottles so I'd have something to buy. Grandma would give me some buttons, and I would pick out my purchases. One time, I lined them all up on the

My grandparents' house in Austin, Texas.

NANCI GRIFFITH

My grandfather's chair, one of the original Barcaloungers,
where it sits in my house today.

counter, and my grandfather made a show of adding it all up and then asked me, "How many buttons do you have?" I showed him. "That's not enough," he said. "You have to put something back."

The center of the house was the living room. And the center of the living room was my grandfather's chair—one of the original Barcaloungers, made of wood. He'd lay back in it like in a cot and chain-smoke Lucky Strikes. And I'd climb up on it and lie against his belly and take a nap. Every day my grandfather would have sardines and pinto beans for lunch. Sometimes after lunch he would tell my grandmother he was taking me to the library. We'd head downtown to Sixth Street, which back then was all old bars and domino parlors. We'd get downtown . . . and we'd spend all afternoon at the domino parlor. When I started school and he took me to the *actual* library, my first reaction was, "This isn't the library."

The house was always filled with music. My grandfather played the piano all the time. He sang in a barbershop quartet. So did my dad—my dad still does. And to this day, when I hear a song, I hear it in four-part harmony. Every song. Truth is, my dad and grandfather would be really surprised if I didn't.

There was never any question that I would become a musician. That I would find harmony in the gentle turn of life. That the love I found in a great big house in Austin would find its way into the songs I write.

Or that if you visited me in my home today, you'd see the most wonderful collection of little porcelain boxes and an old Barcalounger that, even after a complete reupholstering, still smells of Lucky Strikes.

—NANCI GRIFFITH, Musician
Hometown: Austin, Texas

{Mary Hanson}

I loved the big house, which was my husband's boyhood home in Maumee, Ohio, and my home for three years when he went off to war. It was a large frame building, about a hundred years old, and beautifully proportioned in Greek Revival style. It was built as a farmhouse and did not become a town house until the expanding city caught up with it.

My husband's father, Clifford T. Hanson, bought the big house in 1913 when he was a young man starting out in the real estate business. It was originally built in 1835. He had come from Uxbridge, Massachusetts, and the yellow house was not unlike his boyhood home in New England. By an accident of love, courtship, and marriage, my father-in-law had settled in Ohio, a daring departure from family tradition.

It was painted a soft corn-yellow, with white trim and green shutters. It rose with gracious dignity from a large corner lot. Big maple trees grew on either side. There was a flower garden in back and a tennis court was flanked on the street side by a high wall of lilac bushes. On the far side of the tennis court was a chicken house used for a tool shed and the old barn.

At the front of the house was a medium-sized porch, accented with four white columns. A beautifully paneled door, set between narrow leading windows on each side, opened into a wide center hallway. How many times I have seen Papa Hanson opening that door! He was dignified but genial, hearty, affectionate, proud, and possessive. He drew us to him with charm and assurance.

In the wide entrance hall hung a large oil painting of a stern-looking, bearded gentleman, my mother-in-law's father, who had originally come from Concord, Massachusetts, and was a descendent of a Concord Minuteman. Beneath the portrait was an Empire sofa from Papa Hanson's family home in Uxbridge. As Papa would remind you, his mother was a leader in the Daughters of the American Revolution, and many of her pieces, some ugly, some beautiful, filled the house. Also in the hall were two Hepplewhite chairs, a graceful antique sideboard, a huge spinning wheel, a sturdy grandfather clock, and a wide staircase leading upstairs.

In back was the living room, a truly lived-in room. The furnishings were odd and hodge-podge, but the atmosphere was utterly inviting and comfortable. The mantle, tables, and desk were accented with pictures of children and grandchildren. Papa Hanson had his favorite chair. I can see him sitting there, smiling, with the light from a nearby table lamp shining on his bald head, while his wife, whom he adored, sat in her favorite chair and prattled happily about the

Customized greeting cards featuring the
big yellow house in Maumee, Ohio.

children and their doings and the activities and peculiarities of the local gentry. "Men," she once told me, "like to be entertained." Mamma Hanson had been a very pretty, popular, and vivacious girl. She always had an abundance of social charm. Papa Hanson believed in the principles of culture. He had Red Seal records of Caruso and Galli-Curci, and in earlier years he had sung tenor in the Eurydice Club. Mamma H. had no cultural pretenses, but some social ones. She continued to be entertaining and Papa to be entertained.

While his children were still quite young, Papa Hanson surveyed the tennis court out in back. (By training he was an engineer.) When it was built, he taught his boys to play and played with them for a number of years. When I think of the tennis court, I think of pre-World War II weekends, before most of the boys went off to war. I see the sunlight sparkling on the white court and on the young men, tan and healthy, in white ducks or shorts and stripped to the waist for action. I can see the sunlight on the grass, broken by leafy shadow patterns. I can hear the slight whir of the rackets just before the players crunched the ball over the net, and the popping thud of the ball on the court. And above all, I can hear the sound of the players' voices, the brief calls of the play, the absurd insults bandied across the net and the good-natured, rowdy laughter.

Before I was married and for three years afterwards, the clan gathered every Sunday in the

75

dining room for dinner or supper, accumulating in-laws like a ship does barnacles. My mother-in-law spoke often of "The Family" in tones which made it a unit, an indestructible whole. In the earlier days of this family, two grandmothers, two parents, and six children gathered around the grand old mahogany table three times a day. In my mind I can see Papa Hanson at the head of that table. Never did a man so enjoy presiding over a family gathering.

The young people, as Mother Hanson referred to us, had countless suppers and dinner parties in this room, including a memorable wedding reception supper for my husband's sister Helen, who was married a year before Chet and I were. Helen was a strikingly pretty bride dressed in her mother's ivory satin wedding gown. She was like a young queen with her blond groom for a prince escort. There were fourteen of us, ushers, bridesmaids, wives, and fiancées of the Hanson boys, all in evening dress, laughing and talking in a magic circle around the candle-lit table. The table sparkled like a fresh snowbank in the sun, with white embroidered linen, white floral centerpiece, lacy wedding cake, silver candlesticks, and champagne goblets catching the light of the candles. I can see Papa uncorking the champagne, aglow with wine and paternal pride. My husband, then my fiancé, rose to make a toast to the bride and groom. Wedding guests thronged in and out of the rest of the house. I pinched myself to make sure I was really a part of so charming and romantic a scene.

In earlier and more prosperous days, the mechanics of the household revolved around Toma, an exceptionally capable housekeeper. Toma's kingdom was the kitchen, a large sunny room with an ample pantry off it, leading to the dining room. Here she was dictator, autocrat, and warmhearted foster-mother to the young children often left in her care. The core of the kitchen was a huge black, gas range, which Papa had purchased from a hotel supplier. It had two ovens, a broiler, and six burners. Toma needed every inch of it.

When I married into the family, the Great Depression had left its mark here as elsewhere. Toma was gone and Papa himself stepped into the role of chief cook and general steward. He was excellent at it and never happier than when stuffing a huge turkey or basting the Sunday roast.

At Christmas time, the whole family gathered at the big house to celebrate. Best of all was the Christmas Eggnog Party, which my husband had initiated before we were married. The boys, with my husband in command, made a large quantity of eggnog early Christmas morning. It was a serious and intricate ceremony. After the presents were all opened and before dinner was ready, neighbors and friends of the Hansons dropped in. The parlor and living room were crowded. Eggnog foamed from a large Wedgwood punch bowl decorated with blue-on-white pictures of Harvard. Brotherly love glowed from everyone, and the glow carried us well through Christmas dinner. By the middle of the afternoon the house was quiet. Everyone had gone upstairs to take naps.

On rare occasions when the house was empty and I walked through it, I found the rooms alive with the feeling of happy living, unlike some rooms and some houses, which are static and lifeless even when their owners are at home. The rooms were all large and beautifully proportioned. The furnishings and pictures were good, bad, and atrocious. The people were informal, disorderly, often loud, and always warm. They absently wore each other's clothing, and they hung up their things on chairs and on the floor. Bureaus were a magnificent clutter. Once in a while someone took a rake and shovel and cleared out the bathrooms. The boys and their sisters banged doors, walked with floor-shaking assurance, and shouted up and down stairs. Even when the house was empty anyone who had been there much could hear echoes of rapid, clear-cut, happy talk and the heartiest laughter ever known.

And then, just before the war, Papa Hanson died. Soon after, the war smashed the idyll completely. The family was broken up and scattered. The upstairs of the house was converted into two apartments. My husband's mother lived downstairs with a decrepit cocker spaniel for company. The tennis court went to grass and the garden to weeds. The house was shabby and badly in need of paint. Those were dreary days for the big house and the family it owned.

But like an obsolete ship doing honorable duty in time of crisis, it rode out the war years, and better times came again.

The sons returned safely from the war, and with their wives, bought new homes and settled in the suburbs. And in no time at all the big house began accumulating grandchildren, a gay and colorful collection that soon numbered fourteen.

The tennis court became a football field for small boys. Flowers bloomed again in the garden, the house gleamed with fresh paint, and the backyard was once more a picnic ground where on summer evenings children and grandchildren would gather for informal parties, much to my mother-in-law's delight.

Christmas gave way to Thanksgiving as a great family day. Dinner was a community affair, with daughters, daughters-in-law, and old friends all contributing, and my mother-in-law furnishing a huge, golden turkey. Once more the dining room was filled with talk and laughter and shining faces around the big table. Mama Hanson sat happily at the foot of the table, while the oldest son carved at the head. White linen sparkled, silver gleamed, and candlelight glowed. The house was filled with the young children's happy voices and scampering feet. Thanksgiving Day was rich with gaiety and goodness. The big house lived again.

—MARY HANSON, Retired teacher
Hometown: Maumee, Ohio

MARY HANSON

{Rose Heredia}

Mrs. Norwood, the lady next door, had row after row of blooming flowers growing on the small plot of land she called her backyard. I used to watch as her tall frame leaned over that precious little garden of hers and she watered it lovingly with an old, rusty watering can. In our backyard, which was much bigger, pussy willows bloomed each spring. In the summer, patches of juicy figs with thick purple skin appeared on a tree I think my grandfather planted himself, and a rosebush from the neighbors' yard spilled into ours. And way in back, bushes bearing tiny blue flowers grew along another fence separating us from other neighbors.

The thought of that house in East New York makes me think of my best friends back then: my brother, Steve, and our dog, Cleo. The photographs I sift through now show Steve and me cooling off in a one-foot-deep rectangular wading pool and Cleo sitting on a picnic table, a lock of hair falling into her big eyes as she daydreamed—I like to think she was dreaming of ice cream. We used to save the very last drop of our ice cream, the one trapped in the tip of the cone, to give to her. On summer nights, when Dad treated us to Carvel, Cleo would wag her tail and wait patiently until we each got to the end of our cones, then she'd start begging. Who could possibly resist that shaggy brown mutt, the center of our lives, our constant pillow in the living room? Steve, Cleo, and I were inseparable, until our lives changed suddenly.

While the rest of us were crammed upstairs, Grandma used to sleep downstairs in an alcove that we converted into a room with heavy drapes. When she became too sick to climb the stairs, my mom became her nurse, practically sleeping at her bedside. Just before she passed, a priest came to give her the Sacrament of Last Rites, and the smell of incense permeated the house. After she died, our lives quickly changed. Our house was really her house—and it was left equally to my mother and her five siblings, so it

Steve and Cleo.

had to be sold. My father could have taken a mortgage and bought out his in-laws, but he wanted out for other reasons. It was 1961, and Dad thought that East New York was "changing" when two black families moved up the street, claiming that their children had chalked "dirty" words on the sidewalk. The sad truth is, my father was prejudiced, and he thought the presence of these new families would cause our house to decrease in value. Steve and I wanted to stay in the house we loved and become friends with our new neighbors, but we weren't in charge, of course.

Sometimes our childhood shapes us by teaching us what not to be more than anything else.

My father quickly sold the house to the first bidders and rented an apartment in a "better" neighborhood about seven blocks away. The next problem was that our new landlady didn't want dogs. And after a desperate adoption deal fell through, we had only one choice.

My mother and grandmother.

When the ASPCA came, I watched Steve, then just thirteen years old, lift Cleo onto the truck. Without saying good-bye, I went to my room and cried until there were no tears left. Since the life I loved had been yanked away from me, for a while I tried to block out my memories of that house—of playing Cowboys and Indians on the staircase with Steve and hiding out in my bedroom, which was wallpapered with blue ballerinas. But in time, I have learned to treasure those memories and even to understand my parents—if not necessarily to agree with them.

Because I have been a woman and a mother with her own tough decisions to make, I understand better what it meant for my father to marry my mother, move into 50 Milford Street, start a family of his own, and feel responsible for the future of everyone in it.

All those memories remind me today never to run from anything simply because I don't know it or understand it. They remind me to be happy for what I have, to stick it out no matter how tough it gets, and to greet each day with love. Not just for me, but for my family, then and now—including Cleo.

—ROSE HEREDIA, Transcriber
Hometown: Brooklyn, New York

ROSE HEREDIA

{Maria Jaramillo-Bean}

There's something indescribable about driving down the stretch of highway that leads from Ft. Garland, Colorado, into San Luis, Colorado, but every Jaramillo in "La Familia" can feel it. It's a flood of memories, personal yet shared by each of us, spilling out and racing back to mind with every mile. There's a little pink house that calls to us and tells us we're almost home.

It was my dad and his brothers and sisters who grew up in that pink house in San Luis. My grandfather Juan Jose Jaramillo ("JJ" to family and friends) built stucco walls, painted them pink, and placed an iron fence around the front yard to form a protective barrier around his family. That family of ten children and two parents struggled not just to survive, but to live life to the fullest during the 1950s and 1960s. This was a hard time for all families living in the San Luis Valley (most of them Mexican American), trying to eke out a bare existence; a time of great poverty and prejudice.

Me and my brother Gene outside the little pink house in San Luis, Colorado.

I remember a warm house full of cousins and aunts and uncles from all over the States, all of us crammed happily into that tiny home. I remember giggling under the covers at night with my cousins while we "slept" in a row of beds as the grown-ups played cards (rather loudly) downstairs. I remember grandparents who spoke heavily accented English; I remember my grandma ("Goggy" to her grandchildren) praying the rosary and telling me what each bead meant.

San Luis is the oldest town in Colorado and one of the poorest. My dad and his family, along with the other families in the valley, would rise early six days a week during the long harvest season and migrate from field to field, picking the vegetables they could scarcely afford to buy at the market in town. Although there was not much, they never went hungry.

In that tiny house (one thousand square feet) every child ate, sharing one spoon affectionately entitled *la bocarao*—jealously guarded by the lucky user during meals from thieving siblings who would snatch it up if given the opportunity. A wood-burning stove kept the cramped kitchen warm. Too many children and not enough room around the table meant that some had to eat their meals with their plates perched precariously upon their knees, staggered up the stairwell leading to the bedrooms above.

Two small upstairs rooms, warmed by a wood-burning stove, kept ten children warm: six boys in one room, four girls in another. During the winter, a trip to the outhouse during the night was avoided by metal chamber pots, one for each bedroom.

Imagine ten children sharing two bedrooms, one outhouse, one spoon! The stories told about life in that house and the people who lived there are precious treasures to each and every one of us in la familia. We take delight in the great passion that always arises during the telling and retelling of these stories (some of them still hotly debated). All of us cousins never tire of listening and watching and laughing at our parents as they squabble over "who really was to blame" or "how it really happened." That little house comes alive as parents remember and their children imagine the people, places, and events that shaped all our lives.

It was rough, and the outside world was cruel, but every child in that house grew up knowing they were loved and cared for: not an easy task during a time of prejudice against Mexican Americans. Those children overcame great personal obstacles to become the adults I know today: loving, caring people, rich with love of family and heritage.

My father's one of the children from the little pink house in San Luis. His childhood and his heritage are inextricably intertwined with who I am. Who he is makes up who I am; his stories have become my stories. He is a man who rose up on the shoulders of his parents to become the successful and well-respected man he is today. And I am who I am because of him, because of his parents, because of the little pink house in San Luis.

—MARIA JARAMILLO-BEAN, Loan coordinator
Hometown: San Luis, Colorado

{Amy Jasperson}

The story of the house I consider home is the story of my family over a century and a half. The 130-year-old house has been in our family for five generations, built by my grandfather's grandfather Sherman Newell Whittlesey. Sherman bought 240 acres of swampland from the state of Wisconsin in 1871, on which he would establish what is today one of the oldest family-owned cranberry marshes in the country. In 1875, he married a woman named Annie Downs, and soon after they built the house that our family still calls home.

The house was built in three stages. The original part was built in 1876. An addition was completed a year later, and the final portion was added in 1893. Sherman's daughter, Harriet, and her husband, Clarence Jasperson, ran the marsh after Sherman's death and lived in the house part-time until their son, Newell, took over the operation after college. Newell, my grandpa, married Helen Hernlem, my grandma, of Red Wing, Minnesota, in January 1940, and they were the first family members to live in the house full-time. They have lived there for over sixty-five years now and raised three children. My sister, Laurie, and I, along with our cousins, Robert and Kristen, grew up visiting this house and still look forward to frequent visits, especially during the holidays. It was in these visits that I discovered home.

It sits on a beautiful piece of the country and, with no lack of space, as kids we felt no feeling of constraint. Perhaps that's why we loved it so much. To reach the house, we would wind through dense woods down a country road from the main highway to a clearing in the center of the marsh. The house is a large, sprawling wooden structure, white with black shutters, bounded on one side by towering white pine trees. As soon as you step foot on the property, you're struck by the sound of the wind in the trees, the splash of frogs in the drainage ditches, and the chirping of crickets at night in the quiet countryside. The house feels like a cozy refuge from the biting deerflies in the summer and the brutal, icy temperatures in the winter.

The delicious smell of Grandma's cooking floods the house as she bustles around the kitchen preparing the family meals. She would often enlist the help of family members to gather items from her vegetable, fruit, and flower gardens, and by mealtime she would have transformed newly picked berries into a freshly baked pie. The entire family then gathered in the dining room to catch up on the latest. The contagious laughter swept through the house as we listened to Grandma and Grandpa tell stories.

Since it has been home to different people working on the marsh throughout its history, the house has several staircases and multiple living spaces. The original part was closed off and seldom used when Grandma and Grandpa were raising their kids, making for lots of magical, mysterious, and eerie spaces well suited to childhood exploration.

Our family home has housed so many different people in so many different times that we all have different memories of what made it special. Grandpa loved the lively evenings of music in the living room, where family members would sing and play the violin, piano, and saxophone when he was a child. The girls enjoyed playing in the "butterfly room" (named for the butterfly wallpaper) with Grandma's dollhouse from childhood. Today we love to work on puzzles with Grandma in the "Whittlesey room" in the original part of the house or gather in the living room with Grandpa to watch the Green Bay Packers or Wisconsin Badgers play on TV.

The building of our house in Cranmoor, Wisconsin.

While times have changed since Sherman Whittlesey cultivated his first cranberry vines, this house has remained the centerpiece of our family throughout the generations. Regardless of the unpredictability that nature brings each year for the cranberry crop, we can always count on the house to stand strong. Our connection to earlier generations is as much a part of this house as the sticks of wood with which it was built. It's incredible to be part of something much greater than ourselves, something so lasting that it has outlived our ancestors. Its isolated, rural geography created a sense of freedom and exploration and provided early lessons in independence, curiosity, and discovery. We would all grow up with the confidence to strike out on our own, pursuing various professions, and venturing away to different parts of the country. Regardless of our different paths, we all share a common appreciation for Helen and Newell's work ethic, sacrifice, and nurturing.

Their influence remains at home, too, as my cousin Robert fulfills his life dream of taking over the cranberry farm. He and his wife just purchased a house across the yard from our grandparents, and he is preparing to take it all over. So the tradition continues. May it long outlive our generation as well.

—AMY JASPERSON, Political science professor
Hometown: Cranmoor, Wisconsin

{Katherine Jefferson}

I lived on a sugarcane plantation in a tenant house from 1960 until I moved to Pittsburgh after I finished college in 1981. Actually, I lived in two different houses on the same spot—over a few months in 1969 and 1970, our first house was demolished and replaced with one that had an indoor bathroom. Both houses were built by fellow plantation tenants, and neither remains today.

Just about everyone who lived in the tenant homes was part of a large family. People worked hard and were paid very little money. But although everyone was poor, none of us knew it, and everyone shared everything they had with everyone else.

Our tenant home in
Port Allen, Louisiana.

One of the most exciting times of year was the harvest season—we called it grinding. This was when the sugarcane was processed into molasses and sugar. The sugarcane fields would be set afire, which was very exciting for a young girl, and everyone worked longer days—which was pretty exciting, too, because longer days meant extra money.

Our community church was within walking distance of our house. The church was right on the shores of the Mississippi River, and people would cross the levee to be baptized until an indoor baptismal pool was installed in the church in the late 1960s. My father was an associate minister at the church, and my mother sang in the church choir. As we got older, many of my brothers and sisters joined my mother. But as youngsters, we sat together as a family in the second pew while our parents helped to lead services—so we could all be together, but also so our parents could keep an eye on us, I'm sure!

Port Allen, Louisiana, in the sixties and seventies was a small town involved in the early stages of integration of public schools. When I entered first grade at Port Allen Elementary School in 1967, I was one of only three black girls, and each of us was in a different class. My parents talked constantly about taking advantage of the situation instead of being overwhelmed by it. And I don't remember ever being threatened or feeling afraid. The truth is, my early education was a great experience that gave me a strong foundation—I was to complete fifth and sixth grades in one year and entered college a few days before my seventeenth birthday.

Every day I came home to a house filled with noise and love—people talking, a child misbehaving followed by my mother gently scolding, music playing, and someone laughing, always laughing. There were five rooms—living room, kitchen, parents' room, boys' room, and girls' room. Five brothers in theirs, six sisters in ours.

My favorite room in the house was the kitchen. It was the activity center, the dining room, the backdrop for family photos, and, of course, the cookshop. It was always a place of celebration—with so many people, it seemed there was a birthday (with Neapolitan ice cream and homemade pound cake or vanilla wafers) every week.

But nothing was more special than the holidays—Thanksgiving to Christmas. In Louisiana, the best meals start with a roux. Now, a roux's a lot of work, which meant a lot of work for the girls. My mother lined us up, and we started cutting up—cutting up onions, cutting up celery, cutting up peppers, and cutting up parsley. We hated it while we did it, but laughter and chatter made the time go by, and when it was done, it was better than anything.

It was a small house, humble, crowded, and a symbol of everything that could be—of possibility. It was on an unpaved road, and the air was filled with dust, but it was always clean. It looked just like all the other tenant houses that filled the plantation, but it was special. That house didn't shape us—we shaped it. Into a home. And our home taught my brothers and sisters and me that we were not limited by our circumstances; we could transform them and rise above them.

When my parents died in 1983 and 1984, we had to leave that house for good—all of us. Our parents were tenant farmers. They didn't own the house. We could lay no claim on it. But that home had already laid its claim on us—we would make our way in the world, full of love and understanding, and blessed with the knowledge that we could build homes of our own.

—Katherine Jefferson, Engineering manager
Hometown: Port Allen, Louisiana

Katherine Jefferson

{Francisco Jiménez}

Hoping to leave our poverty behind, my family and I emigrated from Mexico to the United States in 1947 when I was four years old. We began our new life as migrant farmworkers, moving frequently from place to place, following seasonal crops throughout California. From the time I was six years old until I was fourteen, my older brother, Roberto, and I worked alongside our parents to help make ends meet.

During those years, I yearned for stability, for a place we could call our own, which came in large part out of a desire to attend school without interruption. I hated missing the first two months of school every year because we had to help our parents in the fields. I enjoyed learning even though school was difficult for me, especially English. To improve my English skills, I kept a small notepad in my shirt pocket on which I wrote English words and memorized them while I picked crops. I took my notepad with me wherever we went. It gave me a sense of consistency, a sense of grounding. I lost my notepad when the migrant shack we lived in one winter burned down. I was devastated. My mother wisely consoled me by pointing out that all was not lost because I had memorized everything written in my notepad. That experience taught me that whatever I learned on my own and in school went with me no matter how many times we moved.

Because I had found a sense of stability in learning, my desire to find a permanent home so that I could go to school without disruption became even more profound. My dream came true in 1957. That year we were forced to settle in Bonetti Ranch, a migrant labor camp, near Santa Maria, California, because my father's back gave out and he could no longer work in the fields. Roberto and I managed to get part-time jobs working year-round as custodians in Santa Maria. We made our home in one of the many dilapidated army barracks that Bonetti, the owner of the ranch, bought after the Second World War and rented to migrant farmworkers, mostly Mexican field laborers. Looking war wounded themselves, the dwellings had broken windows, parts of walls missing, and large holes in the roofs. Scattered throughout the ranch were old, rusty pieces of farm machinery. Located about nine miles east of the city, it didn't even have an address.

Our flat-roofed wooden barrack measured approximately thirty feet wide and sixty feet long. We occupied most of the building, which was partitioned into three rooms opening onto a dark connecting corridor. My parents and sister, Avelina, slept in one of the rooms. My three younger brothers, José Francisco, Ruben, and Juan Manuel, slept in the second room in a twin bed next to mine, which Roberto and I shared. The third room was our kitchen, which had a small narrow window above the sink. We covered the gaps between the wall boards with paper, painted the kitchen white, and replaced the worn-out linoleum with new scraps of different colors and shapes we found in the city dump, making the floor look like a quilt. Along the front edge of our barrack, we planted red, pink, and white geraniums. We were all proud of how we had transformed the old army barrack into our new home. It became our permanent home, the place for which I had longed for so many years. It provided us with shelter, protecting us from cold, wind, and rain and an outside world that at times was confusing and unfriendly. It was a place of welcome and familiarity.

When I left Bonetti Ranch to attend college, I felt homesick. I longed to be with my family again. It was then that I began searching for home in my childhood memories. I recalled waking up mornings to the sound of the rolling of Mama's twelve-inch

Me, outside Bonetti Ranch near Santa Maria, California.

lead pipe as she pressed dough to make flour tortillas and to the smell of chorizo and scrambled eggs. I remembered her gentle voice telling us Mexican folktales that emphasized the value of hard work, faith, and respect. I recalled hearing the barking of dogs in the distance as farmworkers warmed their car engines before leaving to look for work. I could hear in my mind the laughter and bickering of my brothers and sister as they got ready for school, and I could see my father's eyes water as he listened to popular Mexican songs on the radio.

These childhood memories sustained me in college and graduate school. Whenever I felt discouraged and lonely, I would write about my childhood. These recollections became the source of my autobiographies, *The Circuit: Stories from the Life of a Migrant Child* and *Breaking Through*, as well as my two children's books, *La Mariposa* and *The Christmas Gift*.

Besides my vivid memories of shared family celebrations and struggle, I associate our home in Bonetti Ranch with being able to attend high school from beginning to end. This continuity made it easier for me to attend college. And although our barrack burned down in 1965 because of faulty electrical wiring, it now has an address—in my memory and in my heart.

—FRANCISCO JIMÉNEZ, Professor of Modern Languages and Literature
Hometown: Santa Maria, California

{Star Jones Reynolds}

I grew up in a small house tucked away in the town of Badin in the mountains of North Carolina. My grandparents raised nine daughters in that house, including my mother. When they were growing up, there were only two bedrooms, one bathroom, and a kitchen. When my ninth aunt was born, they added on a third bedroom and a bathroom. All nine girls were raised with, at the very most, three bedrooms and two bathrooms—and that included my parents' bedroom. So by the time I came along, it was already a full house. From a child's point of view, it was the biggest house on the planet, but of course, short little kids tend to think things are larger than they are. That house was quite small, but it had a lot of meaning.

My mom was a single mother. She was determined to be able to support our family and was lucky to have my grandparents to help. So during the early years of my life, she went to college and I stayed with my grandparents. They raised me along with my youngest aunt, Evangeline, who was in high school at the time. It seemed such a big job to me. My grandmother would stay at home during the days, occasionally out volunteering or working for charities. My grandfather worked around the clock at the Alcoa Aluminum plant, the big employer in the area that remains there today. I remember seeing him come in at various times with his big black lunchbox, which was typically filled with sandwiches and other little treats. We could almost never tell when he'd be walking in or out. There were three different time shifts: 8AM–4PM, 4PM–12AM, or the graveyard shift, from 12AM–8AM. My grandmother protected his peace and quiet when he worked the graveyard shift; she made us all stay very quiet all day long so he could sleep.

The family house in Badin, North Carolina.

Because the house could be crowded and confining, I spent a lot of time during my adolescent years in our backyard, which ran right up against our neighbors in the back. I also loved the front part of the house because my grandparents had these huge front steps that led up to our porch. And the long road that ran up to the house brings back a hundred memories, but one in particular—one brutally hot summer that road got the best of me. I was a very independent child, and that one summer I was so angry—feeling like no one in the world understood me—that I decided to run away. I quickly learned, of course, that you don't run away in the middle of summer in the South wearing only cutoff jean shorts and a cute little tank top when you live on a gravel road. I got about fifty feet and my feet were burning and hurting so badly that all I wanted to do was go home and get some lemonade from my grandmother. As determined as I was to leave, I couldn't even get down the road. I guess it's harder than we think to ever leave home.

I grew up in the South in the sixties, and you hear so much about racism running rampant, but a lot of the time we were so insulated that we didn't feel it. The first time I felt it was when my grandfather took me shopping to buy black patent leather shoes. We arrived at the store, and there was only one customer in front of us. We waited our turn, but I noticed that people who had come in the door after us were being waited on before us. The store clerk referred to everyone else by their surnames, Mr. Banks, Mrs. Smith, but when he finally got to us (after he had helped everyone else) he called my grandfather Clyde. It may seem small, but that simple lack of respect for a man who worked so hard to take care of his family really affected me. I think about everything I have now and it means so much more to my family because my grandfather had to get through everything he did—Jim Crow Laws, lynchings, separate water fountains, unwelcoming lunch counters, and young white boys calling him Clyde when he deserved the respect of being called Mr. Bennett. Now, interestingly enough, in that town—whether black or white—I'm not referred to as Star Jones or Star on the TV. I'm referred to as "Mr. Clyde's Granddaughter." Finally, after all these years, the respect he deserves.

Home is always there; no matter what, I know that my family will be there—to guide me, behind me, in front of me, to the left, and to the right of me. They surround me, no matter what position I am in. As a prosecutor, I was a victims' advocate. As a televison personality, I still am, especially for children. That's my passion—to give children the wonderful sense of home and family that I was given. I think every bit of confidence I've had in my life comes from the sense of family that gives me my inner strength. Every child deserves to have that.

—STAR JONES REYNOLDS, Lawyer, author, and TV personality
Hometown: Badin, North Carolina

{Anita Koser}

When my single mother brought me home from the hospital, it was to a tiny house on the Lac du Flambeau Indian reservation. The house itself was little more than a tar-papered shack (and torn and tattered tar paper at that) with no electricity or indoor plumbing. But our home was much bigger, filled with a loving family made up of my mother's parents and her fifteen-year-old sister. They more than made up for whatever our house may have lacked in material trappings, and it lacked a lot.

My grandfather used to carry pails of pumped water through the woods and across a field to our little house. We heated and cooked with a wood-burning stove in the kitchen. The floors were

A sketch of our house on the Lac du Flambeau
Indian Reservation, Wisconsin.

rough wood, and splinters were an everyday occurrence. Old kerosene-filled lamps with chimneys blackened with soot provided the only lighting. When it rained, every pot and pan in our house was put into use to catch the drips. We would set our milk on the windowsill to keep it cold. My grandpa grew the majority of our food in his garden and fished year-round in the nearby lake to keep us fed.

Until I went to kindergarten, I didn't realize that people lived any other way. I thought everyone's mother warmed their socks in a wood stove oven before the winter walk to school. I thought everyone learned to read and write, did beadwork, and played cards by kerosene light. I thought everyone's mother worked full-time, and would for her entire life. This wasn't the Depression-era 1930s, this was the late 1950s.

It never crossed my mind that we were poor, that the fact that we didn't own a car, phone, or television wasn't typical of American families at the time. My grandparents and aunt doted on me so much that it was easy to be content with everything I had. I learned early how to love and be loved, and I don't think you can put a price on that. The women in my family never wanted me to feel as though I didn't have the mind or resources to achieve anything that a man could achieve so I also learned to read at a very young age. In books, I discovered the broader world outside the reservation, with many different cultures and lifestyles.

My mother worked as a housekeeper for the wealthiest family on the reservation. This family seemed to have everything money could buy, but the two girls who were my age always begged to come and play at my house! While their home seemed like a palace to me, to them it was the simple escape my world afforded that seemed like paradise. We entertained ourselves by flying kites and searching the grass for snakes.

Back then I didn't know the term "working poor," but that's who we were. But in that little shack we were strong, forward thinking, and sympathetic to one another's needs. Today, as a human and social rights activist, I carry on this tradition, pushing for a universal understanding and sympathy. I'm driven by people like my mother, who never had many options. She just did the best she knew how and gave me a wonderful life. No matter how little we had then, we still found something to spare for others in need.

When I think back to my old shack, I remember a simpler time when people appreciated one another more. I miss those cozy nights of playing cards with my family, and I know that's the kind of world I hope for when I'm fighting for change. And I know now why I never realized we were poor—we weren't. Real wealth has nothing to do with money.

—ANITA KOSER, Human and social rights activist
Hometown: Lac du Flambeau Indian Reservation, Wisconsin

{Delores Leona}

I didn't live in the building I consider to be my childhood home, but it's certainly where I became who I am today. The house on Walnut Street in Wilmington, North Carolina, became a home and a place of healing when my father, Dr. Daniel Carter Roane, moved his OB-GYN medical practice there in the early 1950s. An outstanding diagnostician and chemist, he was widely considered the most talented doctor practicing medicine there at the time. He also happened to be black.

By the time my father purchased the house in 1943, it was nearly eighty-five years old. The two-story Greek Revival home was built shortly before the Civil War by a free black carpenter named James Sampson. A well that still stands in the backyard is said to have been a tunnel to the Cape Fear River used by Confederate blockade runners. After my father bought the house, he converted it into four residential units, one of them occupied by my childhood friend Melvin Wall, Jr. When the Wall family moved out, their first-floor apartment was converted into my father's medical office. The living room became the waiting room, the kitchen an examination room, the master bedroom the consultation room, and the closet a pharmacy. White patients never chose to wait in the lobby with the black folks but instead would enter through the back door or pay for a house call.

Dad's patients came from all walks of life—rich, poor, black, white—and even when some of them didn't have enough money for his services, he refused to turn them away. These folks always found a way to pay him, though, for his medical attention, often with enormous quantities of homegrown produce, seafood, or meat. He wanted his office on Walnut Street to be a welcoming place of understanding and fairness in a time when the country was characterized by hatred and fear. I loved sitting in the lobby chatting with patients while they waited to see my dad and also hanging around in the hopes that one of the nurses would indulge my sweet tooth with one of the lollipops they kept for younger patients. Immersed in this place of compassion, I never realized until later in life what an anomaly that office was, so out of place and ahead of its time.

I was always impressed by Dad's pharmacy, which seemed to contain every medication imaginable. My "brother," Dr. Arthur Lee Stokes, still talks about our father's remarkable sense of medical judgment. He knew his patients so well that he prescribed for them customized medications and he diagnosed ailments without high-tech machinery. Arthur was one of four young men from the neighborhood who joined our family, earning his keep by working around the home and office. Of the six children that my father sent to college, only three were blood relatives, but all are part of the family.

Dad's office sat two doors down from our residence. The neighborhood housed black doctors, lawyers, undertakers, and preachers who would gather regularly to play pinochle. The competition was so fierce that after games it seemed as though some folks might never speak to one another again, but they always returned the following week to settle the score.

When his practice thrived during World War II, a period marked by widespread economic struggle, Father shared his wealth with the community as though that were the natural course of things. Mrs. Audrey G. Wall, Melvin's mother, still remembers with awe the luxury items Dad

A party for the kids and mothers in our neighborhood of Wilmington, North Carolina.

shared with her, beyond scarce goods like panty hose and sugar. He did so much for the town that people happily returned the favor when they got the chance.

My father was a powerful force for racial integration. He successfully sued to integrate the public schools, golf course, and tennis courts. (He was actually an expert tennis player who coached tennis champion Althea Gibson at one time.) His biggest triumph stemmed from what he worked so hard to create at the office—equal medical care for black patients. When he found out that the local hospital continuously dumped black patients into makeshift wards or turned them away without treatment, my father promptly cited the Hill-Burton Act, which states that medical facilities using federal funds cannot discriminate on the basis of race, making sure that all were treated in the hospital as they were in our home.

The house that housed my dad's office no longer belongs to my family, but it stands today as a historically preserved site and a legacy to my father's groundbreaking efforts to uplift the black community. In no other place could I have seen what equality meant, what one person could do, and that justice is something worth fighting for.

—DELORES LEONA, Photographer
Hometown: Wilmington, North Carolina

My father's
office in
Wilmington,
North
Carolina.

{Sugar Ray Leonard}

My dad and my mom were both fighters. They fought for the most important prize of all—a future for me and my five brothers and sisters.

After living in a string of apartments, we moved into a little house on Barlowe Road in Palmer Park, Maryland—to me it was heaven. When we moved into an actual house, I felt like we were the richest people around. The homes were all packed close together, none of them were very big, and just about everybody was working hard to make ends meet, but I was never happier.

My dad had very little education 'cause he had worked the fields in South Carolina with his dad to put food on the table instead of finishing school. He still worked with produce to put food on the table—only now it was the graveyard shift at the S & R Supermarket, where he was the produce manager, and the table was the kitchen table at Barlowe Road.

That kitchen was my favorite room. I can still smell the fried chicken...and the biscuits! The whole family would cram into that kitchen, pretty much around the TV. We'd watch *Good Times* or *The Price Is Right*, and we'd talk. Mostly, we'd talk. And when we were all together, we all seemed to forget how tough life was. No matter how uncomfortable things were, when we were together in that kitchen, even if it was just for a little while, we were all free from worry and at ease.

My mom worked incredible hours, too. Cooking in that kitchen, cleaning, laundry, all the usual household chores—and she worked at Hollycross Hospital, too, doing everything from cleaning to nursing. All their hard work gave us kids the chance to go after our dreams. And it was in that house that I first became interested in boxing. I trained in that house every day, I trained at the football field across the street, I trained at Palmer Park Recreation Center. I trained hour after hour, day after day, for years. I remember running to school instead of taking the bus—and being laughed at by the kids on the bus when it drove by. But my parents taught us to fight for our dreams—and my dream was a big one. I wanted to go to the Olympics. I wanted to win it all.

I will never forget how it felt to come home from the 1976 Olympics with the gold medal, walk through the door, and see all my family and friends there to welcome me. I was home.

My parents taught us to go after whatever dream was in our hearts and to go after it 100 percent. That's how they went after their dream of giving us a good life, and they won the gold.

I miss that old house in Palmer Park.

—SUGAR RAY LEONARD, Former professional boxer
Hometown: Palmer Park, Maryland

Our house in Palmer Park, Maryland.

{Maya Lin}

Iwas born and raised in a house in the small

college town of Athens, Ohio, and I have returned to that home for the holidays every year until last year, when my mother decided it was too large a house for her alone. I have always considered myself lucky to be able to come back—and to rummage through the same closets filled with my childhood stuff. And then, once I had children, I loved being able to bring them home and to share my childhood home with them. Especially since both my parents had emigrated from China, I always wondered where home was for them while I was growing up.

The house itself was nothing special, but its setting was unusual. Even though it was in the town proper, it was completely hidden from view and quite rural in character. It was set way back from the street and surrounded by deep woods. The driveway was tree lined and long enough so that very few Halloween trick-or-treaters ever ventured near.

The house was a traditional-style structure that my father had renovated himself to increase

My house in Athens, Ohio.

its size so that it comfortably housed our family of four. My father's renovation—though done on a shoestring since both my parents were poor academics—was at once comfortable and modest, yet it reflected a modernist and craftsman's aesthetic. From the enormous picture windows that opened onto views of woods to the furniture, a lot of which my father had made himself, there was a fifties modernism that had a distinctly Asian character: clean lines and love for simplicity. This house and my father's design has had a strong influence on my own aesthetic.

Equally important to me was the wooded setting. The house was set in a small valley situated between steep ridges. Three streams flowed from the hills behind the house, coming together in front of the house in a small ravine. My brother and I spent a great deal of our time playing outdoors in this incredible backyard. Whether we were chipping at the rock ledges that flanked the driveway or playing in the woods and streams behind the house, we were always connected to nature. There was also an abundance of wildlife here, from songbirds to raccoons to deer.

I think that most of my work has been inspired by and connects back to landscape and natural phenomena. How we relate to the land is something I am continuously exploring in my work. When I think about my childhood home and surroundings, I guess that's not a surprise—it's something I've been exploring my entire life.

—MAYA LIN, Architect
Hometown: Athens, Ohio

Our secluded driveway to the house.

{Ileen Linden}

My childhood lives forever in a house in the Shaker Heights neighborhood of Cleveland, Ohio. I grew up there with my parents, my three sisters, and my grandparents Tillie and Isadore Morrison.

Tillie and Isadore were a source of wisdom and comfort throughout my childhood that I still draw on today. Their life together is a story of courage, faith, and unyielding love passed on through a legacy of rich storytelling. Many a time, Grandma would lift me to her lap and fill my head with visions of her and her sisters picnicking in the mountains of Romania, prior to immigrating to America in 1890. I didn't have to imagine her young, as there were many photographs of her as a dark-eyed beauty. She was a petite woman paired with my educated grandfather, a tall, handsome young man. Their story in America began on a boat to Ellis Island, she barely twelve years of age and he a boy of just seventeen. Stacks of letters tied with blue ribbons remain as proof of their early love. Reading these letters brings forth tears and laughter, all the many faces of life: Tillie's sorrow at losing her young brother to the flu epidemic, Izzie's jealousy at hearing of Tillie dancing with "another man" at a party while he was housed in quarantine for TB, both awaiting the marriage of Tillie's older sister so their own betrothal could commence. Their words leap from the pages of handwritten history.

By the time I was born in 1953, Tillie and Isadore were proud owners of a lovely two-family English Tudor–style home in Shaker Heights. My grandparents occupied the upstairs suite, while my parents squeezed our family into the downstairs suite. The two stories were adjoined by staircases, one in front and one on the side, and you could always hear children's heavy footsteps running and jumping up and down through the two suites. The two-bedroom apartment downstairs could not accommodate all four children, so my oldest sister eventually took one of the third-floor bedrooms, while the other was reserved for many a female "boarder," a welcome source of extra money. Whoever the boarder was at any given time was welcomed as part of the family, joining the kids (if they dared) for meals, conversation, and even politics in Tillie's kitchen.

We were a sight—seated all in a row upon a C-shaped upholstered bench in the kitchen nook! I can still smell the pot of chicken soup on the stove and hear Grandma chuckling at the sight of us as she passed the plates filled with little odd dishes from her country: bananas with sour cream and smoked whitefish and eggplant, cooked directly on the stove burner. We didn't question it; it tasted good to us!

At holiday time, my sisters and I would help Grandma carefully set the table with her best china and glasses in preparation for the arrival of the "aunts and cousins," young and old, some arriving from as far away as New York City. Their arrival was always special as we anxiously awaited the sound of new footsteps climbing the stairs. When the door swung open, shouts of excitement rang out. We found their accents fascinating. The children teased one another: "It isn't aw-range soda," we'd tease, "it's or-ange pop!" Together, we would sit at the big dining room table stretched to capacity, with the "children's" extension added onto it. We would all have a little wine, or at least a little taste for fun, anticipating what we knew would be the biggest dinner yet with more courses than we could count: soup and salad; beef, chicken, and turkey; stuffed baked potatoes; cookies and cakes. Every family has its cook, but, hands down, our grandmother was the very best; her recipes were kept secret for many years until they were passed down as prizes to my sisters.

I remember love, but I also remember sorrow. My mother's only brother died from cancer when I was three years old. He and my grandfather ran a produce business together. Sanford, as the only male child, was my grandparents' pride and joy. Although I don't remember him, Sanford's death seemed to linger within the walls of the Rolliston house. Grandma could never talk about him without great sadness and flowing tears. Even at such a young age, I could sense that a part of Grandma died with Sanford.

My brother Dale, with my sisters
Sandra and Lois, and a cousin.

Ileen Linden

Our Shaker Heights, Ohio, home.

But my mother, a beautiful, artistic woman, worked hard to take care of us, to help out upstairs, and to remind my grandmother of all the joy that remained. Grandma didn't drive, but she certainly liked to talk, so there was always conversation in the Buick that Grandpa drove. I would stretch out on the long backseat, listening to Grandma's opinions about the day's events. Mostly I remember how much she cherished education, especially teaching. She wanted all the girls to be teachers, a vocation she valued as the highest of goals.

I loved my grandma dearly, but I adored my grandpa. Well into his seventies during my childhood, he still stood straight and tall in his "uniform": a brown suit, hat, and cigar. He never failed to greet me with huge open-armed hugs and big pockets full of candy, wrapping his long arms around me, lifting me high "to the sky." He was my best friend, who was also the "surrogate" grandpa to all the kids on my block.

One night, just after a wonderful party at Rolliston, Grandpa kissed us all good night, complaining of a headache and deciding to go to bed early. Little did we know, as we continued playing and talking, that this would be the last time we would see him. That night, he died peacefully in his sleep. Grandma, once more dressed in black, called us kids, one by one, into a now darkened living room. This time it was she who wrapped her arms around us, giving us each the wonderful gift of our personal story: the ways in which Grandpa loved us "best" and how we would always remember him.

I've returned only once to Rolliston, long after the house was sold and under new ownership. It still stands, as pretty and welcoming as I remember it. But, truthfully, it is difficult for me to visit as an "outsider" to the house I loved so as a child. Inside and out, the Rolliston house was a garden, cultivating the values for a new generation of children as they moved to adulthood. It takes only these profound words of Tillie herself to describe the everlasting effect of those years:

> *You have many questions to ask. Very few questions in life are answerable, but there is one question I can and will answer. You asked, or said, that I don't want to move, so here is your answer. . . . Your beloved mother and father, young and with great hope in their hearts for all of you, were here to add so much to my great joy. Your loving mother with her kindness nurtured the rose bowers, and many beautiful flowers stand about with the children. With your mother's kindness, everything was alive and blooming. This is the reason for my holding on.*
>
> *With love and affection for all my dear, dear sweet grandchildren, I am thankful to God.*
>
> —Taken from a letter written by Tillie shortly before her death

—ILEEN LINDEN, Adjunct professor
Hometown: Cleveland, Ohio

{Kathy Mabry}

Throughout my life there has been one place
I could rely on no matter what—it was built in the 1830s by one Colonel Buford of the Confederate military. My home since I was born, it's a place with an open door and an open invitation to return for everyone in my family, no matter when or why you left.

My parents, eight siblings, various in-laws, and I have all lived in the house, each long enough to get on our feet. You have to understand that Daddy never let any of us go without. If you needed food, he would provide it. If you needed a place to live, he would provide it. No explanation needed or even wanted. He was just happy to provide.

The foyer, a wide hallway with a beautiful winding staircase at the end, was lit by an old carbide lighting fixture (now converted to electricity) that hung at its center. Just off to the left of the hallway lies the bedroom where two of my siblings and I were born. Daddy didn't like hospitals because he irrationally feared that one of his kids would be mixed up in the nursery and he would bring the wrong "young'n" home. In those days, you could convince a doctor to come out and deliver a baby in the privacy of your own abode, so all nine children were born in the house.

As the youngest of them all, I was always in awe of the constant "comings and goings." We rarely locked the front door, so friends and family flowed steadily through the house at all times. Everyone kept different schedules, and Mama served as a kind of short-order cook. The heavy, warm aroma of fried chicken, pheasant, and vegetables from the garden drifted through the house from the kitchen, perhaps the reason people were drawn there as a gathering place. When visitors came by, everyone sat around our big table sipping a cup of coffee with whoever happened to be there. Of course, Mama was always there. The kitchen was always occupied from early in the morning until late at night. When you were looking for someone, it was wise to check the kitchen first because that's where the action was. I spent many nights at the table trading stories, laughing, and crying with loved ones.

With a brother and sister in local bands, our musically inclined family often threw impromptu concerts. Friends would frequently stop by, and before I knew it I'd hear the sound of guitars coming from the living room. And when I needed to be alone, I escaped to my bedroom, even though I shared it with my adored older sister, Beverly. I would sit in the windowsill reading, with a cool spring breeze blowing in from the orchard that sent a sense of calm through my bones.

Entrance foyer and spiral staircase with carbide lamp.

KATHY MABRY

Our home in Kentucky.

The house sits on a four-hundred-acre farm outside of Midway, Kentucky, a town founded and built by the railroad company in the nineteenth century. We were tucked into the heart of horse country, where many farms specialized in raising Thoroughbred racehorses, many of whom made it to fame. During the fifties, sixties, and seventies, Midway was like Mayberry. A main street with a railroad track ran through the middle of town, flanked by exactly one of everything: one barbershop, one grocery, one drugstore, one hardware store, and, well, three churches, but only one of each flavor: one Baptist church, one Disciples of Christ church, one Presbyterian church.

Everybody knew everybody, which meant there were no real secrets, and when anything notable happened, word traveled fast. This intimacy also blurred class lines, especially in a place where everyone shared, even if some families had more than others.

I moved out of the house in 1981 to live on my own, an important "declaration of independence." The house became home once again when I moved back for a couple of years with my husband and newborn son. We never had a true neighborhood growing up, but later in life we managed to make one of our own.

When the first of nine kids was married in the 1960s, Daddy began the tradition of giving each child an acre of land on which to build a house. We saved for a house of our own and in 1988 moved into the new place built on the acre of land that Dad gave me. At one time, eight of us (and our spouses) lived in a row of houses along the southern property line of the farm. I lived between my oldest brother, Edward, and my youngest brother, Larry. You may think that having my brothers as territorial bookends would have been "too close for comfort," but we managed to respect one another's privacy while enjoying the uncommon intimacy of our own family village. Behind our row stood the house we all called "home," the lighthouse of our tiny community whose lamp burned into the night with our night-owl mother. Our bodies grew, but our idyllic lives remained intact, and that made us all stronger.

Mama and Daddy passed on a few years ago, but the institution of family life they created lives on today. We are all one another's security blankets, and the circle will never be broken because our parents built it to last. Today I'm a full-time wife and proud mother of four children, striving still to be like my parents: always there.

—KATHY MABRY, Mother and homemaker
  Hometown: Midway, Kentucky

{Schylar Meadows}

I've lived in the same two-story structure since I was seven years old. Only one other family has lived here in the house's eighty years. When we first moved in, my parents lived downstairs and the children lived upstairs. And that's how it still is today—I'm upstairs and my father lives downstairs.

The design of the house is simple—a rectangular body with a triangular roof. When we first moved in, it seemed so big that I thought it was a skyscraper. A sturdy tan wooden torso sits atop squat brick legs. Inside, the basement is concrete, the upper levels are hardwood, and the doorways are all lined with careful woodwork. Light pours in through windows in every room, flooding the house with sunlight regardless of the season. You can tell the weather by the sound of the wind, whipping through bare branches in the winter or softly rustling through the leaves in summer.

The kitchen isn't the largest room in the house, but as in so many homes, it's certainly the most utilized. If you followed the aroma of fresh coffee that my mother would make in an old-fashioned percolator, it would lead you here. If you followed my father's morning routine of

My home in Toledo, Ohio.

packing up a lunch on his way to work at the plant, it would lead you here. If you followed the noise of guests chatting after holiday meals, it would lead you here. Today, I sit at the kitchen table to help my nephew with his junior high homework.

We live in metropolitan Toledo, Ohio, a blue-collar town that enjoyed its greatest prosperity when the "Big Three" automakers thrived. And while we struggle with job creation and housing costs like many industrial towns, our strong city leadership, fine metro parks, and nationally known art museum and zoo make Toledo feel like a town of hope.

We live within fifteen minutes of almost every part of the city, and our neighbors have hardly changed since my family purchased the home more than forty years ago. The close bond between families who have been part of each other's lives for at least two generations is palpable, and we can't imagine finding such a deep sense of community anywhere else. We have celebrated weddings and graduations together, had block parties, worshipped together, and voted together. We have mourned losses and helped each other through tough times. Our neighbors all come from different backgrounds and do different things, but they're all important, from the mayor two blocks away to the firefighters, health care workers, factory workers, educators, veterans, and retirees who all live side by side and share each other's lives.

After years of growing up in a place where community gave and meant so much, I decided I wanted to give something back. In June 1993 I stood on my front lawn and announced that I was running for Toledo City Council. I had sent press releases, invited my neighbors, and practiced my speech. I was barely in my twenties and very nervous, but the reassuring faces of my neighbors gave me confidence. With everyone gathered in the yard at 7:30 PM I walked to my "podium"—the second stair of the squeaky front porch—and delivered my first political speech.

That night summed up what home means to me: gratitude for the place you call your own, a sense of responsibility for being raised there, and a commitment to make it better.

Living in this house has shaped my sense of community, responsibility, and character. Our home is not just a place we live, it's a family legacy. I developed understanding, tolerance, and compassion for the human experience from being a neighbor—but more important, taking stock in being part of a community. As a health care worker, I now devote my life to helping others make their lives better. I also take my message from that second stair to the radio as a public affairs talk show host. All of this, everything that I do now, began in my home. I thank God and my parents for giving me such a good one.

—SCHYLAR MEADOWS, Health care worker
Hometown: Toledo, Ohio

{John Mellencamp}

I can't pick just one house—because I grew up in two very different environments that each left an equal mark. Until I was thirteen, I lived right in the center of a small town, and then we moved out into the country. It wasn't quite city mouse and country mouse—but it was sort of town mouse and country mouse.

My first home, a brick house on West Fifth Street in Seymour, Indiana, provided an unbelievable amount of other children to play with. After all, it was the baby boom, and it seemed there were ten kids in every house down the street, which allowed me to have many relationships with young people my age.

The community was so close, there was an open-door policy. I can remember going into people's homes when they weren't there and helping myself to soft drinks and just leaving a note that said I had done so. "Hey, I stopped by and got a Coke, John Mellencamp." The old adage, it takes a community to raise a child, was definitely the rule in that neighborhood. I received verbal punishment from other kids' parents, and that was okay, because everyone knew and trusted one another.

Yeah, I loved growing up on West Fifth Street, but in 1964, when I was thirteen, we moved

My first house in Seymour, Indiana.

Our home on top of the hill in Rockford, Indiana.

into a house out in the country. It was in a town, if you want to call it that, called Rockford, Indiana, a place with great history, so they say. The first train robbery supposedly took place there, and a band of hooligans called the Reno Brothers burned down the town of Rockford to ensure that the railroad would go through Seymour.

So by the time we moved to Rockford, there was only a small grocery store, an arts-and-crafts shop, and a church. There weren't hundreds of kids running around the way I was used to, but the house was on top of a hill, which at least meant I got better radio reception. FM radio had just become popular, and my parents made the mistake of buying me one. At night, I could pick up stations all the way from Waco, Texas, to Chicago, Kansas City, even as far as New Jersey. So while my parents were sleeping, I was listening. I was experiencing the music of America.

I shared my love of music with one kid who lived about half a mile down the road. He was into the wavelengths, but I was into the music. He and I became good friends, and we toiled away our time in the summer almost like Tom Sawyer and Huckleberry Finn. That guy is still a good friend of mine today.

So I had twin childhoods. And I think you can hear that in my music. I certainly feel it in my bones, and today I feel at home in both—the quiet dignity of life along the rural route and the warm company of life in the heart of town.

—JOHN MELLENCAMP, Musician
Hometown: Seymour, Indiana

111

JOHN MELLENCAMP

{Cheryl Mitchell}

Building a great house takes a great set of plans, but building a great home takes much more. Starting with the blueprints in 1961, my family built every inch of our home, our character present in every single piece of it.

The house was built in Nissequogue, New York, a North Shore village naturally rich with abundant woods and beaches. Once a huge estate belonging to the Otis Skinner family, it was divided into parcels of land like ours for new, rural housing.

The saltbox structure was meant to connect the house to the surrounding woodlands my parents cherished and to showcase the books and curiosities collected during my grandfather's world travels. From furniture to floor coverings, all the decor was hand-crafted by our family. The house was rich in burnt umbers and barn reds, with braided rugs handmade from vintage suits discarded by the wealthier side of the family. We dug our own wells for water and built this lovely home with our own hands, largely because of Dad's emphasis on working to our fullest potential, buying quality materials, and adding to it as money permitted.

Each day Mom put on the kettle for tea as the clock chimed four o'clock, and the wind soughed through the summer pines while the tea was transferred outdoors. Music ranging from Goodman to Chopin to bagpipes always hummed in the background. Pine crackled in the huge fireplace at the far end of the kitchen–family room (rigged with Dad's ventilators to disperse heat throughout the house and save fuel), while everyone performed their tasks all over the house to different sound tracks. Dad played Glenn Miller in his woodworking shop as my brother strummed his electric guitar with the amp turned off. Mom and I cooked and cut out fabric to sew whatever article of clothing was needed at the moment, with our endless conversation ranging from all the places we longed to visit to why John was a better songwriter than Paul.

In the heated 1960s, the house served as refuge where we could discuss the decade's ideas but keep its turmoil at bay. It showed little evidence of the revolutionary times around us except for the occasional blare of the Beatles and Cream and my Dad's innovative devotion to the environment. (We used only fallen wood for our fireplaces and paved our driveway with cracked scallop shells abandoned by the tide.)

A gloriously large table in the kitchen–family room welcomed all to the heart of the house. Dad had fashioned it from the former sign of a men's clothing shop—and didn't hesitate to tell everyone when they remarked on its beauty. More important, it was a table of firsts: where I

Our home in Nissequogue, New York.

witnessed politics in action for the first time when Dad and his friends lobbied successfully to block the construction of a bridge across the Sound; where I learned to cut fabric properly on its broad surface; where we held the first of many holiday gatherings and fiercely competitive games of double solitaire.

My father's values were built into every brick and beam of that house, but also into the framework of my life. Championing the belief that women could do anything, he taught me woodworking and wiring as the house took shape. The book-lined walls, thick with histories and the great novels, were my first grasp on the power of the written word. In those woods and our handmade home, I developed the sense of place that drives my stories and makes them my own.

— CHERYL MITCHELL, Writer
   Hometown: Nissequogue, New York

{Meredith Moon}

My father was in the Navy, so we traveled a lot when I was young. One of my first memories is from my early years in China just before the Japanese invaded, and digging up a twelve pound rose quartz rock on Coronado Island. During World War II, we lived in Arlington, Virginia. I remember the rationing of shoes and sugar, helping the war effort by collecting scrap metal and newspapers with my red wagon, and the deep sense of pride and purpose with which a seven-year-old spent her ten-cent allowance on war stamps. The Arlington house is where I remember opening the front door to a Navy chaplain who had come to tell us that Dad had died in battle on August 5, 1944, defending his country. I was ten; my brothers were eight, six, and four. Arlington was the last house where we had our father and the house where we leaned on one another after he died. There were many houses before and many houses after Arlington, but this was the house where my character was formed.

Dad was a rear admiral who had commanded Force U—the amphibious assault on Utah Beach at Normandy—on June 6, 1944. Before that assignment he served on the staff of Admiral King, the chief of naval operations, and had rented the Arlington house from an employee of the Federal Reserve, who had moved his family to Richmond when the Federal Reserve was relocated there during the war. The Arlington house was three stories tall and a basement deep. In the basement was a coal furnace and next to it a huge pile of coal. My brother Don had the job of keeping the furnace stoked. Though twenty months younger than I was, it did not seem unusual to us then that a boy *so* young had such a huge and difficult responsibility. He also never made it seem like a big deal—it was his duty, and he took pride in it.

The living and dining rooms and the kitchen were on the first floor. A radio sat next to our father's chair in the living room. Through its speakers, we heard all the war news, the *Lone Ranger*, and *Jack Armstrong, All-American Boy*. The living room furniture included pieces mother had collected during our years in China. I was particularly fond of the Coromandel screen behind the sofa.

My bedroom was on the second floor; my bed had the most unique history. The four-poster bed had been carried by covered wagon during early pioneering days from Virginia to Kokomo, Indiana, where my father grew up. My parents' bedroom, right next to mine, and a sleeping porch for the summer months that opened from my father's small office took up the rest of the middle floor. The stairs to the finished attic led from my room to the two rooms above where my brothers slept.

Our Arlington, Virginia, house.

Meredith Moon

Despite our family's many moves, my mother always managed to make our home beautiful wherever we were, often with her own small additions. In the backyard of the Arlington house, she built a goldfish pond surrounded by a terrace. We helped her by carrying all the smaller stones out to its site. My brothers also built a wonderful submarine out of scrap wood for make-believe games of "going to sea." And it was in the long, narrow side yard that dad taught us how to hit a softball.

Arlington is a residential town, with amenities for families like the small park I passed each day on the walk to school and on summer days accompanying my father to his bus stop. My friends and I rode our bikes anywhere we wanted and played safely at our neighbors' houses, but the feeling of war in the world beyond our playgrounds still hung over all of us. In school, we had air raid drills where we all crouched under our desks until the all clear was sounded. And the war wasn't the only thing to provoke childhood fears—there was the polio epidemic. I remember my fright when the first child I knew was hospitalized. The next year my brother David caught bulbar polio. Before recovering, he had to be hospitalized in an iron lung.

I vividly remember learning in that house a lesson that would guide my adult life. One summer I found a featherless newborn bird in my bicycle basket, took it inside, and built a cardboard home for it on the sleeping porch next to my bed. I cut up worms and ground hamburger meat to feed it throughout the day, beginning at 4 AM. Eventually the bird grew feathers—its red breast showing it to be a robin. When it was old enough I taught it to fly, starting with a gentle push from the bottom step of the front porch. It finally grew strong enough to fly away. The next summer, a full year later, it came to me once to sit on my shoulder, and then I never saw it again. It felt like he just wanted me to know he was still alive and flying. That experience of selflessness and love for one who could not survive alone meant so much to me at that young age. In a way, that robin would be perched on my shoulder my entire life.

The Arlington house was filled with love—from our parents, between siblings. It was the house where my father taught me to reach my full potential in everything I did. It was the house where my mother gave us poetry, art, and a sense of noblesse oblige. It was the house where my sense of compassion grew, where I gained an awareness of human vulnerability, and where my courage to do what is right, whatever the personal cost, took shape.

Years later, at twenty-one, I stood in a hallway of the neurological ward at D.C. General Hospital in my first job as an occupational therapist. To my left was a ward of quadriplegic men on striker frames; to my right a ward of men suffering from severe brain damage. I knew that day that I must find confidence and strength that does not rely on knowledge or physical skill, since both can be lost to us in an instant. I understood well what life in the Arlington house had taught me so many years before—that the human condition is vulnerable, that little in life is truly assured, and that I must use my time here in ways that matter at a soulful level.

In my forties, I decided I wanted to make the inner journey to psychological and spiritual maturity easier and safer for others. I earned my Ph.D. in depth psychology studying the work of C. G. Jung at the Institute in Zurich. In the years since I have had the privilege of being with many others as they journey within themselves to find who they truly are. I believe we can heal the world by helping each other. I've held this belief ever since my family learned how to heal by embracing each other, back in Arlington.

—MEREDITH MOON, Psychotherapist
Hometown: Arlington, Virginia

{Yvonne Morrison}

The story of my home is the story of my father's dream house. Not just my story; it's our story.

My father was born in a log house in 1936 in Blairsville, Georgia. While growing up in the north Georgia mountains, he visited lots of folks who also lived in log houses. And he loved the logs of the old tobacco barns that sprinkled the countryside of the North Carolina farm country we lived in.

So in 1977, when I was twelve years old and he was forty-one, despite never having built a home before, my daddy set out to build a house made of tobacco barn logs—because he loved the log houses he remembered from his childhood, and he wanted to preserve the old logs of the barns where we lived. Before he was done four years later, he would buy and tear down thirty-one barns and three log houses. This is the story of our home, the House of Many Barns.

Since Daddy worked full-time, construction on the house was mostly a weekend project. The first thing he had to do was salvage and preserve the logs from the barns he had purchased. Using a backhoe from his pipelining work and his own old logging truck, Daddy and a few helpers would carefully take down the logs, haul them to Daddy's land, and run them through his sawmill. He would leave the hand-hewed sides as they originally were and cut the logs evenly on the other two sides. Since the spaces between the log rows were not chinked with cement, the logs needed to be even on two sides to sit on top of one another. The interior walls, made from different types of wood, were constructed from lumber Daddy cut down, ran through his sawmill, and hammered into place. He even hand-split the oak shingles in the gables with an old-timey mall and froe.

The rest of the family helped build the house, too. My mother and I would staple strips of insulation on the top row of logs. Then Daddy, often single-handedly, would wrestle the next row of logs into place. He would drive a twelve-inch spike into the logs to secure the row to the one below. Once the walls were up, Daddy sandblasted the logs to reveal their natural wood color. He stained the logs to preserve them.

Daddy has always had his own way of doing things. Since the logs were historic, many over 150 years old, Daddy did not want to cut them up to make way for windows and doors. He always said that he could not bring himself to cut more holes in the walls than were absolutely necessary. After the log walls were up, Daddy took a chain saw and cut the windows and doors where he wanted them.

Building the house was certainly a labor of love, but it was also a test of his will and grit. In 1980, just as he was finishing work on the house, the recession hit and Daddy's pipelining company went under. Daddy did not declare bankruptcy, although he probably should have. Instead, he pressed on against record interest rates and hard times, laying one log at a time, fixing one stone at time, hammering one board at a time. He was determined to finish his home. He even built several pieces of furniture, including tables and curio cabinets. If I didn't know better, I'd say Daddy has sawdust running through his veins.

We moved into our log home in 1981. I asked Daddy to describe what he sees in his house. He said, "I see old farmers out there chopping logs to build their barns and trying to put their tobacco up. I see mules dragging logs in so the farmers can hew them and build their barns."

The house is full of special features: a cathedral ceiling, stained-glass windows, log staircases and rope trim. Most people who visit Mom and Dad have the same reaction when they walk in: They are amazed at the beauty and craftsmanship of this home. They can't believe Daddy conceived of and built the house himself. The huge log beams in the living room support the tongue-and-groove pine ceiling, lumber Daddy cut and sawed at his sawmill.

The House of Many Barns, North Carolina.

119

Yvonne Morrison

Moving the House of Many Barns to its new location.

The rock fireplace is a focal point of the living room and is where Daddy would frequently cook a pot of stew or bake potatoes in the hot coals of the fire. And we always had a nice fire going in the cool weather. The smell of wood and the popping and crackling of an ever-present fire are soothing and comforting. When I'm stressed or upset, sitting on the stone hearth in front of the fire seems to make everything okay.

I will never forget Christmas in 1988. The county historical museum asked Mom and Dad to put our house on the Christmas home tour. We had to put the tree up in late November and have all the decorating done in time for the tour, which was held the first weekend in December. Daddy hung kerosene lanterns outside each window, and we hung one of his mother's handmade crocheted snowflake ornaments inside the window. The house was breathtakingly beautiful.

The day of the tour was bitterly cold. Since the other houses on the tour were on the other side of the county, we wondered if people would brave the weather to come see our house. We shouldn't have worried!

The first folks must have spread the word of the log house in Mebane because it became the "must-see" of the tour. The wind was blowing, and Daddy had a roaring fire in the fireplace. People would come in from the cold and park themselves in front of the fire and not leave. The tour was supposed to end at 6:00 PM that evening, but we still had people sitting in front of the fire well into the night.

It was amazing how people would come into the house and touch the walls, rubbing their hands along the rough logs as if recalling a distant time. They lingered over the ornaments in the windows and asked us to give them a tour and describe how the home was built.

"This is a house that you can feel comfortable in, whether you're in a tuxedo or overalls," says Daddy. "I have always felt good about coming home to it, and I was always glad to see it when I got home."

My parents still live in the House of Many Barns—although that took some doing! In 2002, they and all their neighbors sold their land to developers. But my parents weren't about to give up the house they built with their hands. Instead, they had the entire house picked up and moved. Now that's commitment.

Growing up in that house made me appreciate my family's mountain heritage. I understood what Mom's and Dad's lives must have been like growing up in the Appalachian Mountains, where often many of the houses in the community were made of logs. I discovered that, like those old logs, sometimes people who are rough and worn on the outside are valuable and beautiful if given the chance to stand tall and proud.

—Yvonne Morrison, Owner,
corporate apparel supplier
Hometown: Mebane, North Carolina

Our dining room.

{Judi Patton}

Hibbard Avenue is in Pike County, Kentucky,

where both my paternal and maternal great-great-great-grandmothers found refuge from the march of the Cherokee on the Trail of Tears. Our home was a modest brick two-story that sat on the corner. In 1950, like many streets in America, Hibbard was filled with hardworking people, rearing their families, going to work, sitting on their front porches, and feeling so safe that they never locked their front doors.

My daddy, Roy, was sheriff of Pike County. He was elected on a platform to clean out bootleggers and stop the corruption that spoiled the reputation of our beautiful mountain town. My mama, Esta, cared for their four daughters: me, my older sisters, Anna Ruth and Colleen, and my younger sister, Nancy Roy. At night on the front porch, Daddy would begin stories that sometimes took many evenings for him to complete, making them up as he went along.

On July 28 of that year, as we were tucked in bed, Daddy received an anonymous phone call; a man with information on a case asked to meet him. Mama begged him to wait until morning, but he felt the need to go. He left our front porch and walked down the sidewalk to his truck, and we heard shots ring out. We ran to Daddy as he lay dying, and Mama cradled him in her arms. Our struggle to live without him began that warm night under the lamplight, a journey that would shape my life.

Mama took over for Daddy and became the first female sheriff in the town. She stood firm in the battle against bootlegging that cost Daddy his life. But the factions that feared my father rallied against her when she ran in a special election to complete his term, and they defeated her.

Of course, they didn't stop her commitment to raising her family right and helping others in every

Clockwise from top left: Anna Ruth, Colleen, me, and Nanci Roy.

Our home in Pike County, Kentucky.

way she could. She opened a grocery store, where we were expected to help after school and on Saturdays. Even though we were struggling, Mama offered credit to women and families who needed help. When the store eventually closed down, she never attempted to collect from them.

She completed college and became a social worker. Her "fieldwork" required traveling many miles to visit families. Sometimes it was necessary to go by boat to reach them. She would return home late, often bringing women and children with her. We shared our evening meal and abandoned our beds in order to offer comfort to those strangers in need. When we complained, Mama reminded us, "Girls, you just don't know how hard some women and children have it."

It was those words that rang in my ears when I became First Lady of Kentucky in December 1995. I learned about the honor of public service and commitment to others from Mama. She was my inspiration and the reason I was determined to be a voice for women and children who were not heard in the state capitol. Many times I addressed the state legislature about topics that just a few years before were taboo, such as preventing and punishing child abuse and domestic violence. My knees often shook, but I knew the message was more important than my anxiety.

Life's journey takes us down many roads. I was often asked why I chose women and children. My reply has always been easy: "I am the daughter of a social worker." Our lives were forever changed on Hibbard Avenue; my mama's strength and courage gave me the inspiration to do my part to change the lives of others for the better.

—JUDI PATTON, Fundraiser and consultant
Hometown: Pike County, Kentucky

{Catherine Pease}

In Coventry, New York, the farmhouse where I grew up still stands on property that Grandpa Bickford purchased in 1925. When my grandparents and their seven children moved in, the wood-shingled home had already survived two generations of families. It stands at the top of a small rise, overlooking the state road as it ran south to Harpursville.

As a teenager, Dad worked as Grandpa's farmhand, struggling with the rocks in the soil and being there when he upgraded the farm with a steam tractor. As Grandpa got older, Dad took over the farm chores. Dad, Mom, my sisters, and I lived in one-half of the nineteen-room farmhouse while my grandparents lived in the other half. In 1948, Dad officially bought the farm. He and his brothers built what we called the "little house" for Grandpa and Grandma on farm acreage a short ways down the road.

With Dad needing all the help he could find, my grandparents' old half of the house soon filled with farmhands and their families. My dad had three girls and no sons, so we also became Dad's farmhands—milking, haying, baling, bringing in the cows, and filling the huge silo with silage. Needless to say, our house was always full and busy.

With twelve-foot ceilings inside and a gabled roof outside sporting a brick chimney that spewed the smell of coal smoke on brisk winter days, the two-story farmhouse was a wonderful home. Softened snow dropped from the shingled porch roof to the stone pathway. Every summer, pink, red, and white hollyhocks grew between the sidewalk and the attached garage. And our bountiful garden ensured we would never go hungry.

On hot, steamy days, we pumped the handle of the bright red water pump in our backyard until spring water gushed from the spigot as we ran under it, screeching with delight.

On windy days, I would remove Grandma's thick quilt from the chair on the back porch, wrap it around me, and then run, jump, and roll under the branches of the huge old pine tree. I'd lie there listening to the sounds of nature while winds whistled above me.

During the years I lived there, the township reeled from economic depression and war, yet we were tight-knit and relied on our neighbors in times of hardship. As the most successful farmer in the area, my dad felt a strong obligation to share what he could with the other farmers.

In the summer of 1951, Dad purchased a thresher for the harvesting of our corn and oat crops. It was the only such motor-driven machine around, and Dad determined that surrounding

Bickford farmhouse.

Bickford barn.

farms would have access to it when it came time to harvest the fields. "Have thresher, will travel" became more than a TV catchphrase for us.

My older sister, Jan, and Dad moved the thresher from farm to farm while the farmwives cooked hearty lunches for the workers to eat. When one farmer's crops were stored for the winter, the thresher, the farmhands, and the farmwives moved on to the next. It was a true example of what cooperation and sharing can provide.

We went to a one-room schoolhouse through our elementary years and then off to the "big" school on a bus after the morning chores. After Jan went to college, I finished high school and then, in 1959, went on to college. Although I never officially lived in my farmhouse again, I've never really left home.

Dad always said that "without his farm girls" he would have to sell the farm, and in 1959, he did. Everyone pitched in and helped build a smaller home for Mom and Dad on a three-acre plot of land just down from Grandpa and Grandma's "little house."

Today, the farmhouse stands empty and somewhat the worse for wear. Yet the home I grew up in remains alive in my memories, its imprint always apparent in my writing.

—CATHERINE PEASE, Retired educator
Hometown: Coventry, New York

{Fannie Phillips}

My childhood home was a simple five-room house, but it was home to sixteen people: my parents, my thirteen siblings, and me. It rested in Madison County, Georgia, on a farm of about two hundred acres where we grew cotton, corn, and cane and raised chickens, pigs, and cows. Today, the house is gone, but the foundation stands—and our whole extended family still gathers under its protection every June.

I grew up during the Depression, a time when our land and our produce were not worth enough to make ends meet. My father was a sharecropper, and when our landlady died she willed us the home, but until then we didn't even own the farm ourselves. Neighbors helped one another both emotionally and financially. The local pastor came by every Sunday to drive us to church in his car. His only income was the tithes he accepted from church members in the form of syrup and chickens. It was a town where money had no bearing on someone's worth, because love came first and there was much more of it.

It was a rickety old house; I loved the kitchen, where my mother taught me to cook. Every year we made cane syrup to spread on freshly baked biscuits. There was a constant supply of fresh milk and butter: We churned our butter in the house, and the milk came straight from the cows. We were completely isolated from the world outside our rural community other than the times we gathered around the family radio with neighbors to hear the Grand Ole Opry or the Georgia Jubilee. We lived without electricity until 1945, since we seemed to get along just fine without it.

We would occasionally gather around the fireplace in the living room (the only one in the house) to tell scary stories. Every night, my father and mother would gather by our beds to pray with us, sometimes even teaching our overnight friends prayers as well. Spending so many good times together made our family strong enough to survive the tough times. For example, my family really stuck together during the year I was very ill. I broke out with large sores all over my back and legs, and we could not afford the health care I needed. When the doctor finally came, he didn't think I would survive and began to come more frequently as my condition worsened. My family had to pick up my slack on the farm because I wasn't allowed in the sunlight. After missing a full year of school (which I worked to make up), I finally got better. I'm not sure what would have happened to me without the help and loving arms I found in that house.

I was the only one of my parents' fourteen children to graduate from high school. Because I

What's left of our house in Madison County, Georgia.

was the youngest daughter, my older siblings thoughtfully sent money to my parents to help with my education after they left. Since they had all been working, they knew then how important an education was, even when it was an uphill battle to earn one. My father would not allow my younger brother to attend school out of fear that he would be drafted into the army upon graduation to fight in World War II (which had begun while he was in high school). For my brothers and sisters, it was very difficult to get to school. Our teachers, unable to see the societal changes afoot, would often tell us that we didn't need schooling in an agricultural economy. Also, it wasn't until I was in school that buses came out near us, and even then I had to walk some distance to catch one.

Through the example of my parents, whose actions—not just words—showed the principles of Christ, I became a strong Christian myself. We have revivals each year to help young people learn about God and give them the opportunity to be baptized. I believe that the combination of a life with so little money and so much faith gave me strong morals to stand on and a will to work hard enough to overcome whatever hurdles I encountered in my life. I cannot imagine how I would have turned out without the teachings of such a compassionate home.

Today I am seventy-five years old. I look back on my life and remember our family home as the most beautiful place on earth. The house caught fire in 1970, but as I said, the foundation remains—on this earth and in our hearts. And when we return to its shelter each June, we are all reminded that even if things turn to dust around us, we'll always have the strong foundation of home, made of love, unity, and faith.

—FANNIE PHILLIPS, Retired sewage plant worker
Hometown: Madison County, Georgia

{John Rehfuss}

My daughter and I grew up in the same city and wanted to share our memories together. Two generations, two houses, one home.

Like my dad said, we wanted to tell our stories together. Here's how it looked from my end. At six in the morning the door would ease open. My dad would start to sing, "Oh how I hate to get up in the morning. Oh how I hate to get out of bed." Depending upon how much sleep I had, a laugh or groan would issue from beneath the covers. When I got older, he switched to knocking gently on the door to make sure we were up. Always kind, always gentle. Like a soft breeze that you miss when it's gone.

Unless snow fell the night before, the clomp of horse hoofs on the bare street awakened me and my brother every morning. Our room was situated at the front of our house in Albany, New York. We'd get up and start our day by running down the stairs of our two-family home to pick up the bottle of milk. We had cars then, but some items were still delivered by horse. If we were lucky, we'd be able to watch the horse flick his tail as he clopped down the long boulevard.

Dad arrived home every evening at 5:40 pm with his briefcase in hand. Pulling off his coat, he'd call out, "I'm home," and head immediately into the kitchen, where he'd find Mom fixing dinner. He'd encircle her waist, and for a moment they were the only two people in the room. He held her, kissed her. It was as if he started the day working toward this one moment in time. Eventually, Dad loosened his tie as he glanced over Mom's shoulder to see what she had cooking in the pots on the stove, and he would always have a kind word to say about what she was preparing.

Father would generally get home around 5:00. He was part owner of a foundry/blacksmith shop, so he worked quite hard there, while mother kept the house together at home. Because lunch wasn't available at schools in those days, not only did she prepare breakfast and dinner, but our lunches every day as well. I can still recall the smell of the chili sauce she made on days it was particularly cold.

As he wound his way to the bedroom to change, he'd seek out each one of his nine children. We could be found in the family room watching TV, in the living room reading a book, studying in our bedrooms, or playing a game. He'd find each one of us to ask about our day. What did we learn? Who did we meet? The more people you meet, the more you experience. The more you love. The more you enjoy life.

The house in Albany, New York, where John grew up.

131

The neighborhood was important in my day. You knew everyone on your own block and several streets over. You know, if pressed, I could probably tell you where every kid in my neighborhood wound up living, who they married, what they did. We were connected from the day we met, and time only strengthened the bonds.

He had a habit of allowing you space, encouraging an opinion, and making you feel ten feet tall because all the time—all the times I stumbled and fell, bounced off the walls, slammed a half-thought-out opinion into the mix, or railed with unwarranted emotion—I knew, always knew, that he had faith in me.

Everyone was required to be at the dinner table at 6:00 pm sharp. No excuses. It was a lively atmosphere. Dad or mom would throw out a topic, and we'd debate and discuss and eat and debate and discuss until someone would finally suggest we play a game. In the summer, we'd rush outdoors for a game of baseball, touch football, tennis, basketball, or badminton. Dad stands 6'3" tall and commanding. He had been one of the Wonder Five players for the local high school basketball team, so he taught us a thing or two about the sport, but no one was as good as he was at placing the ball in the net.

Kids all over would skate down the street which intersected with our boulevard. My two brothers, sister, and I would join them from sun up to sun down. That is, if we weren't riding our bikes or tossing a baseball through the makeshift hole we made out of canvas on Mr. Leonard's property out in back of our house.

It was years before any of us knew what Dad did for a living. He was Dad, the one who got us up in the morning and made sure we got off to school on time. He was the one who drove us to the dances, to the movies, to the baseball games, the one who would call home to see how we were doing when we were sick. He was and is a charismatic storyteller. If he didn't have one of his stories to share, he'd read us a bedtime story after kneeling with us to say prayers before going to bed. He took us skiing, swimming, bowling, fishing, tobogganing, or out for ice cream, making sure we always had something to do. In the car we'd sing songs, play games, debate life's issues with a fever. Every Sunday we'd go to church, have a huge breakfast after mass, and often took drives out to the country.

Church was central in our lives. Ours was located just a few blocks down the street, and we'd walk to church alongside other families—the best time of the week. With the stock market crash that became the Great Depression, the imminent threat of war, and only rudimentary prescription medication available, we found solace and in our church.

Always, always, always…. He cared. He cajoled. He praised. He encouraged. He pushed. He prodded. He loved so deeply. He taught so wisely. A gentle bear of a man we would say to others. A magnificent man we would hear back.

He was a lawyer who spent most of his time performing pro bono work for the elderly, orphans, teens who had lost their way. He was a judge. He is my father.

I majored in physics in college, then decided after the war to practice law. I must have done well on the boards, because a Supreme Court justice asked me to work with him, but I went another route. I tried to set aside time to help those in need. I can't say I saved the world with my pro bono work, but I think I eased some folks' burdens. For six years I worked as a city court judge and hope those who came before me felt they were treated fairly.

I remember sitting in the second seat of our large station wagon. It was late, the sky a black velvet backdrop for the stars overhead. We had just spent the weekend at the World's Fair in New York City. I stared up at the stars, night dreaming. Click. My dad turned on the radio and quickly adjusted the volume knob to insure no one would be awakened by the noise. He glanced to his right: Mom and Kerry were still sleeping. Looking in the rear-view mirror, he could see Jack, Peter, Linda, and Sue sound asleep in the third seat. He checked the road. Again, he checked the rearview mirror. Nancy, Elaine, and Stephen were asleep in the second seat. Then he caught my eye and smiled. I smiled back. He returned to the task of driving his family safely back home. I returned to the task of being a kid on a long ride home with the safe, secure knowledge that I was loved and everything was all right with the world.

For me the room that holds the most memories is the dining room. This is where we'd gather as a family to eat a meal, hold a discussion, or listen to the radio. You have to remember, TV wasn't invented yet so the radio captivated us. Besides, the dining room was important to me from the very beginning…with the help of two doctors and a nurse, I was born there!

I don't know what else to say, yet there will always be so much more to say. He is everything to me. He's eighty-five years old. Still noble, still distinguished, an honorable man. John W. Rehfuss. Dad.

I've been a fortunate man. I grew up in a loving household with many cherished childhood memories. I've been blessed with great friends and was fortunate to find that a blind date with a wonderful woman, Patricia Howley, would become our lifelong marriage. Together we raised nine children. I look back and am amazed how quickly time has flown.

—JOHN REHFUSS, Former attorney and judge
  Hometown: Albany, New York

{Narciso Rodriguez}

My parents, originally from Cuba, arrived in the United States in 1956. After living for a year in a furnished one-room apartment, twenty-one-year-old Rawedia Maria and twenty-seven-year-old Narciso Rodriguez, Sr., could afford to move into a modest, three-room apartment I would soon call home.

In 1961, I was born into this simple house, situated in a two-family, blond-brick building in the Ironbound section of Newark, New Jersey. Within its walls, my young parents created our traditional Cuban home, the very heart of which was the kitchen. My parents both shared cooking duties and unwittingly passed on to me their rich culinary skills and a love of cooking that is still with me today (and for which I am eternally grateful). Passionate Cuban music (which I adore to this day) filled the air, mixing with the aromas of the kitchen. Here, the innocence of childhood, the congregation of family and friends, and endless celebrations that encompassed both, formed the backdrop to life in our warm home.

Growing up in this environment instilled in me a great sense that "family" had nothing to do with being a blood relative. Quite the contrary, our neighborhood was made up of mostly Spanish, Cuban, and Italian immigrants at a time when overt racism was the norm and segregation prevailed in the United States. In our neighborhood, despite customs elsewhere, all of these cultures came together in great solidarity and friendship. It was a close-knit community of honest, hardworking immigrants who extended a hand to people who, while not necessarily their own kind, were clearly in need.

Our landlord and his daughter, Alegria (my babysitter and first friend), lived above us, and Alegria graced our kitchen table for meals more often than not. Also at the table were Sergio and Edelmira, my surrogate grandparents who lived in the basement apartment. (I would not know my "real" grandparents, Narciso the Elder and Consuelo, until 1970 when they were allowed to leave Cuba.) My aunts Bertha and Juanita and my cousins Arnold, Maria, and Rosemary also all lived nearby and regularly joined us at our table. Countless extended family members came and went—and there was often someone staying with us temporarily until they were able to get back on their feet. My parents always kept their arms and their door open to the many people we considered family, knowing that they would do the same for us.

My mother and father had come to this country with such courage, without any knowledge of the language or the culture. They came selflessly, as many immigrants do, to give their children a better life, even though it meant leaving behind their families, friends, and careers in the country they loved. They struggled both personally and financially, braving the harsh northern winters while yearning for their native tropics and facing cultural hardships. The barriers to work were strong and high, and my parents both had to accept that they might not be able to find the kind of jobs they deserved. In Cuba, Narciso, Sr., had worked in a laboratory and Rawedia Maria had studied chemical engineering. In the United States, they had to start their lives over entirely, taking whatever work they could find. The faith that this struggle would lead them and their children to better times drove them to endure these hard times.

Me, at our house in Newark, New Jersey.

I will always be grateful to my parents for their love and sacrifice. I've often told them that what they did was a much more courageous thing than I could have ever done. I've often told them of my admiration for their strength and perseverance, and I've thanked them repeatedly. But, in reality, there is no way to express my gratitude for the spirit of generosity impressed upon me at such an early age and the demonstration of how important family and friends are. These are two lessons that my parents did not just tell me. They showed me with their lives, and these teachings have been the basis of my life.

It was in this simple house that my parents welcomed other refugees to celebrate their arrival to this country and where I celebrated my first birthdays. It was in the warmth of the kitchen in this humble house where a Cuban feast (albeit a frugal Cuban feast) always filled the air with not just scent and music but life and love. It was here where I learned the real definition of "family." And for this, I will never forget that house or its gracious neighborhood or the many things I learned there about how to love. I will never forget how my parents turned this simple house into a home.

—Narciso Rodriguez, Fashion designer
Hometown: Newark, New Jersey

{Sarajane Sein}

I grew up in what I consider to be our greatest family heirloom. My mother lived in our house for much of her childhood, and before that, my mother's father lived there. My father moved into the house when he married my mother, and I am still here today. Since my mother's death in 1990, it's just been my father, my brother, and me.

It's an average-size home, and its yellowish tan coat got a makeover when Dad painted one part white several years ago. A lovely dogwood tree grows in the front yard. Inside the house, we have an indoor porch whose door opens into our living room.

The living room, the family hub, is decked with a sturdy old stereo, a trampoline for my brother, and a TV whose antenna we have to put on the floor on nights we want to watch *Amazing Race*. (We're "in between cable companies" right now, so it's always a feat to get a good picture.) This is also where we hold video game competitions and conduct our weekly Saturday Trivial Pursuit matches.

Then there's the dining room, not really appropriately named since we haven't actually dined there in a very long time. Instead, the dining room table is home to a stack of books I've been reading (right now it includes *Gone With the Wind* by Margaret Mitchell and *Franny and Zooey* by J. D. Salinger). Next to the table stands our life-size cardboard cutout of President Bush, which I bought in Philadelphia's subway mall. (It was a tricky task getting him home on the subway!) Our old computer also sits on the dining room table, and even though it's plugged in, it hasn't been used in a while. (Upstairs we have our new computer in an actual computer room with equipment and a bookcase. The door to the computer room is strung with those hippie-style beads.)

Then there's the kitchen, which smells every Saturday and Sunday morning of cappuccino. We have a sort of weekend morning tradition and wake-me-up—on Sundays we sip our cappuccinos and listen to *Breakfast with the Beatles* on the radio.

Collingdale is an ever-changing town only about a half hour outside of Philadelphia. Right around the corner from us is a trolley stop, and since we don't have a car, we get a lot of use out of the trolley. There's also the often frequented Wawa right around the corner, where I can always get sodas and hoagies. Collingdale is one of four towns that make up our school district, so I attend high school in the next town over.

When I was younger, I was one of only two girls on our street; everyone else my age was a boy, so I quickly developed a talent for roughhousing and wrestling games. The guys used to come over to my house to play Sega Genesis, or on nice days we'd go outside and play tag (not my strongest sport) and capture-the-flag. I learned the hard way what ABC gum was and never to accept it. (For the record, it's "already been chewed.") After a while they all moved away, and now my best friend and carpool companion, Connie, lives around the corner in an apartment next to her family's restaurant.

It's strange to consider that I'm eighteen now and my house has been a part of me for my entire life. Most people I know have lived in multiple places, but I've only lived here. I've developed a sense of belonging that will make my transition to college next fall a real change. I have a connection to it, and our family has history here. Every inch of the house has a story behind it, and that's something I'll never forget. This is where my dreams of becoming a writer first materialized, and the dream lives on today.

This house has been passed down through my family, so I don't know if I'll end up raising my own family here, but I know that wherever I end up living, I will always try to make it what my house was for me growing up—a place where I knew where everything was, where everything had some sort of meaning, and where we all, always, belonged.

—SARAJANE SEIN, Student
Hometown: Collingsdale, Pennsylvania

Our home in Collingdale, Pennsylvania.

137

{Jamie-Lynn Sigler}

Sometimes it feels like we grow up too fast

or life moves so quickly around us that we're not even sure how we got here in the first place. But then we remember: it all started at home. For me, home is a midcentury house in West Birchwood, a cozy neighborhood tucked into the community of Jericho, New York. I moved in with my parents, Steve and Consuelo, and my two brothers, Adam and Brian, in 1984, and we changed the house a lot as soon as we moved in. Sometimes my mom and I still drive by when we're in the neighborhood, sad to see that the new owners have painted it a different color.

Kids and dogs were constantly running around the neighborhood's streets and grassy lawns. My friends and I made quite the gang, riding our bikes around to different houses pretty much every day after school. Of course, when it started to get late or dark, Mom would get in the car and come searching for me to usher me home. Busy roads bordered the neighborhood, so we couldn't venture far, but we never had trouble finding plenty to do within its boundaries.

It was a tight-knit community—I had friends on almost every block within the neighborhood. When we got our dog, Randi, that meant meeting even more people, because Randi made friends. One woman had two dogs, Bichon Frisées, and we used to set up playdates for her dogs and Randi. (It was comforting to know that any time Randi ran away, we'd know where to find him!)

Our house was like a magnet, with people always coming and going. People always complimented us on the way it smelled—my mom took incredible care of it and was always burning candles and incense to make it inviting. Your first instinct upon walking into the house would be to jump on any of the couches or chairs and make yourself at home. The walls and tables, covered with picture frames (just like my home now), were a constant reminder of our memories and filled the room with joy. No matter what time it was, noise always filled the background. Whether it was chatter or someone practicing the drums, quiet simply did not exist in our house, but the noise was a familiar comfort. You get so used to it, you can't live without it. Everyone in my family still listens to the TV in order to fall asleep—when I was growing up, there were different channels blaring all over the house as people got into bed!

During the warm months, our house was always packed because we had a great backyard and happily hosted people on a regular basis. Between my brothers and me, there would always be friends over for pool parties, and on weekends my parents often threw barbecues or family gatherings. Those are the times I've missed the most since we moved out. Since I am five and

My childhood home in Jericho, New York.

eight years younger than my brothers, we all had different school and social schedules, so the house got chaotic at times. But Mom always made sure that when we were all home (and not at sports practice, dance class, auditions, or on dates), we ate dinner together. Despite our hectic lives, it always felt easy and important to find the time for those dinners.

Aside from the kitchen table, we always gathered in the den. With an enormous wraparound couch and big TV, it was the coziest, most relaxing room in the house. We held all of our holiday parties and birthday celebrations there, and we spent lazy days and sick days there, too. To snuggle up to the fireplace in winter was simply heaven. The den was also the set of all our home movies, back when my brother went through his director phase. In fact, starring in three sequels of *Commando* made me decide to pursue acting seriously. During my first season on *The Sopranos*, when I was still in high school, my friends and I would huddle on the couch in the den on Sunday nights, order pizza, and watch the show. It's funny to realize that it came full circle, back to the den.

My experience in that house really established my love and appreciation for family and friends. We didn't need to do anything or go anywhere to have a good time. It was all at home for us. And I will always know that no matter where the future takes me, home will always be where it started.

—JAMIE-LYNN SIGLER, Actress
Hometown: Jericho, New York

{Elizabeth Spencer}

My childhood home makes a living impression—like our family, it was strong in character and always standing tall. My mother's father built the house on his farm in 1904. His wife died young, and he was left to raise three children. As my grandfather aged, he had a lot of heart problems and could no longer take care of the farm alone. Since my mother was the oldest daughter, we moved into the house with him.

As you approach the farm along the dusty dirt roads of Adair, Missouri, the house appears on the horizon, a small vision in white. Through the ornate iron gate in front, a soft green grass carpet leads up to an impressive circular porch with solid round pillars. The front steps seemed to invite us for a seat, where we could enjoy some watermelon or homemade pie on a summer's day. Sometimes we'd watch my dad and my sister Mary do cartwheels on the front lawn. But neither the house nor my dad were frivolous types. When you live on a farm, you have to "make hay while the sun shines." That meant a lot of hard work in the fields, the barn, and the garden. Our house was just an extension of the farmland around it, always connected to one another.

The distinctive house had a front parlor used only for special occasions, a living room, a large

A watercolor of our house in Adair, Missouri.

kitchen-dining area, bedrooms, and a bathroom that my parents added. In the back sprawled plum trees, apple trees, and a very large garden that we all helped to tend, even though my father thought he was the only one who could plant straight rows.

Everyone typically gathered around in the kitchen, especially with all that good food which came straight from the garden. On Sundays, after attending the Catholic church in town, we'd have big family dinners. The house smelled of freshly baked bread and rolls my mother always had waiting for us upon returning from our two-and-a-half-mile walk home from school. My mother also canned everything—vegetables, fruits, even meats—so that we'd have only good old homegrown food.

My father grew up in the town of Marceline, about sixty miles away from Adair. Once he became acclimated to the farm life, he became one of the strongest members of our community, often in demand because of his talent for repairing machinery. At threshing time, the men all helped each other, while the women prepared huge meals for them. As independent as we were, in many ways we relied on our neighbors as if they were family.

On that farm we all learned a good work ethic; we all had our jobs to do and were responsible for our own lives. But we took care of each other, too. I've always remembered the day my mother bought me a beautiful fuchsia coat; she needed it more than I did and we didn't have the money for two, but she wanted me to have it. Mother was always doing things like that for others. In the evenings she used to play our organ and sing to us. On warm nights, I'd sit with my father on the step of the porch, singing old songs and staring up at the stars.

After leaving the farm and starting a family of my own, we returned often to visit. My children loved playing among the hay bales, feeding the lambs with baby bottles, sledding across the frozen pig pond, and pretending to drive broken-down farm machinery. The farm offered acres of freedom and joy that most children will never know.

After my parents moved from the farm, we all missed it dearly. We missed the familiar sound of the screen door closing, the aroma of fried chicken from the tiny kitchen, and the taste of cool well water sipped from an enamel cup. Yet we always remember the closeness of our home's cozy rooms warmed by a wood stove in winter that brought our family together, and made us feel safe and protected. We've carried that feeling with us throughout our lives.

Like our home, my family has weathered many storms, but we are still standing. Today, I live in Florida near three of my children and six grandchildren in a beautiful home that my youngest son built. Although my life is here now, a part of my heart will always be in Missouri.

—Elizabeth Spencer, Mother of five
Hometown: Adair, Missouri

{ Steven Spielberg }

I was born in a Midwestern city and spent my early childhood in the New Jersey suburbs, but I grew up in the Arizona desert.

My father was an electrical engineer who designed computers and data processors, and we moved around every time he got a better job. So in 1957, when I was eleven years old, my mother, my father, my three little sisters, and I moved to a cowboy town called Scottsdale where my parents had built us a home. It was a small split-level house set right on the floor of the great Arizona desert, just two miles from the foot of Camelback Mountain.

Now, to get a picture of what growing up in Scottsdale in the late fifties was like, you need to put what you know about Scottsdale today out of your mind. It wasn't a booming oasis of golf and tourism and luxury homes. It was a dusty town of a few thousand people and one paved street that had only been incorporated seven years before. Don't get me wrong—it was wonderful, but it was just starting. I grew up in Scottsdale, and I got to watch Scottsdale grow up, too.

Our home was one of the first houses built on the development property, and for the first year it really was like living out in the desert. But houses quickly started to sprout—across the street, next door, on the other side of the alley behind our house. Grass started to grow—there was a berm around the lawn of every house so it could be flooded from irrigation ditches and give the grass a chance to flourish. Orange trees were planted and began to flower on every yard of every home in the neighborhood. Soon, the smell of orange blossoms was everywhere and the sound of doves and quail outside our windows would wake us in the morning.

Our dusty desert town wasn't booming yet, but it was blooming.

Our house itself was small and compartmentalized. There was a kitchen and breakfast room, a living room, and a small den on the first floor. Down the hall was a master bedroom with one bathroom, three smaller bedrooms, and a communal bathroom at the end of the hallway that my sisters and I shared.

My bedroom was my private place; the kitchen was our gathering place. The den was a rumpus room, and the living room…well, the living room was covered in plastic and pretty much off-limits except for special company. Of course, when those special occasions did come by, it was exciting. The plastic covers came off the furniture, the plastic runners came off the white shag carpet…and we were all on special notice not to trample around in dusty shoes or muddy boots!

As quickly as houses sprang up, there were families to fill them—and they were all like ours.

Across the street, down the street, behind us, and next door were families with kids our ages. With dozens of kids in the neighborhood and the Arizona desert as our communal backyard, we had a permanent cast and a magnificent stage for every game we could dream up and every adventure we could imagine.

It didn't rain often in the desert, but when it did—it was Biblical. And when it did, we had the movies. Scottsdale Road was the only paved street; all the side streets were tamped-down desert clay. When it rained, they turned into a messy, muddy quagmire. We'd plow through the mud on the ride into town, and settle into the Kiva Theater. And then we'd watch two features, ten cartoons, an episode from a serial, and previews for coming attractions. We'd take all the fun and memories home with us and leave nothing behind but mud under our seats.

Running around in the desert or spending a day at the movies wasn't the only way we got to set our imaginations free. Arizona was where I made my first movie, *The Last Train Wreck*, with my father's 8-millimeter Kodak camera and my electric train set. It's where I made my first World War II movie, *Escape to Nowhere*, and where my first full-length movie, *Firelight*, gave me my first premiere at the Phoenix Little Theater.

Scottsdale is where I learned what was really important to me—family, memory, and imagination. That's what home is about, too. It's a house that is touched by all the living souls who share life under its roof, the memories that have helped to shape them, and the dreams they hope to shape. It's about the scent of a family—its ups and its downs, its accomplishments and its setbacks, the good grades we celebrated and the bad ones we tried to hide, the unhousebroken pets, and the noisy room where everybody fought over one of only two telephones in the entire place.

A house is a container for your living memories, and those memories never go away, even long after the family that once called it home has moved on and its rooms are occupied by strangers who now call it a home of their own.

—STEVEN SPIELBERG, Movie director
Hometown: Scottsdale, Arizona

My childhood home
in Scottsdale, Arizona.

{Barry Switzer}

I was raised in the country, out in the "sticks," some of my friends called it, as though I were deprived of something. But I never knew or felt that. I simply grew up in an old country home in south Arkansas in the 1940s and 1950s with my mom and dad, my little brother, Donnie, and my grandparents; I knew no other life. As I look back upon those years, I realize that other children born around 1937 did not have certain advantages that I had and that it was they who were actually "deprived." And I say this because the way my family lived was a tremendous learning experience that made it so much easier for me to identify and feel at home with people from all backgrounds—especially with those who grew up as I did or those who were really poor. You see, I was close enough to those folks who lived in or near poverty, both African American and Caucasian, to know and understand all about it.

My mom and dad were not "dirt poor," but because of where, when, and how we lived when I was a child, I learned how those who were dirt poor did live. The actual home and the outbuildings associated with my youth, which had once been part of a working farm, had a lot of learning in them.

For almost all of my life, my brother and I have each been telling our friends that we grew up in a "shotgun house." But my brother, Donnie, recently did some research on the Internet and found out that, technically, our home had been a "dogtrot house"! It turns out that "shotgun houses" were really dwellings provided for slaves back in the early South, but of a design still popular in the South of the early twentieth century. But in the twentieth century, unlike in earlier times, they were usually found in cities such as New Orleans, Little Rock, or Charleston for housing poorer people. The reason the descriptive term *shotgun* was used was that if someone were to stand at the front door of one of them and aim a shotgun at something behind the house, since all the doors of the two or three rooms lined up in a row, the pellets would pass all the way through the house and not hit anything!

But our "dogtrot" was even more interesting. Like the "shotgun," it had its roots in the terrible days of slavery, but it became a design that was popular and almost pervasive in the rural South of the early twentieth century. Such homes were characterized by a long central hallway running down the middle of the structure—originally designed so the dogs could stay out of inclement weather and so that the natural breeze could circulate through the structure. These houses would have rooms, as many as three or four, on each side of that long middle hall. That is precisely the type of house we had, but it was gussied up, made a little fancier, by a porch that went across the entire front of the house and one side, and it had doors at the front and at the rear of the long central hall. On the right side was the "living room," filled with a daybed against the interior wall, a really big fireplace on the outside wall, two outdoor lawn chairs, a Victorian marble-top table with a kerosene lantern and a chair of some sort, and a table with what was—to us, at least—a huge battery-powered AM and shortwave radio. My granddaddy had strung a wire through a number of the dozens of large oak trees between the house and the county road some

A sketch of our house in southern Arkansas.

one hundred yards away to act as the shortwave antenna, and I spent hours at night as a little kid listening to football games and baseball games, and my parents would as well. Of course, they also listened to President Roosevelt in the earlier years.

There was also a dining room on the right side of the hall with a round oak table and chairs, a cabinet built into the wall for my grandmother to put the "nice" dishes in, and a battery-powered telephone on the outside wall. I am sure it was the only one around out in the country, and it had a single line that my granddaddy had strung on poles and trees through the woods all the way to town in Crossett (just over two miles). Back then, in the 1940s, people had telephone numbers like "37," "56," or something like that. But, of course, since the operator knew everyone in town, you could just ring her up and she could connect you to whomever you wanted.

By the double outside windows in the dining room was a daybed where my dad would spend much of his time watching our driveway so that he could see his customers coming up to the old house to buy his bootleg whiskey. You see, while our dad had several different businesses in his life, the one thing that he found brought in an income upon which he could depend was selling untaxed liquor that he would get in Mississippi or Louisiana and bring back to Ashley County, Arkansas—which was "dry."

Behind the dining room was the kitchen, which had a table with a red-and-white-checked oilcloth covering it and six old ladder-back chairs. There was an old wood stove that my granddaddy and daddy kept going all of the time—especially in winter—but it was also the only way that any cooking could be done regardless of the time of year. In the wintertime when we had to go to school, my dad, who would have been up for hours, would get my brother and me up, and we would grab our clothes and then run down the long hall to the kitchen to dress by the wood stove. There was an "icebox" (not a refrigerator) for keeping fresh milk from the cow, butter, and certain other foods cool. Ice was delivered once a week in blocks of five, ten, or twenty pounds— whichever was desired. There was a sink for washing dishes and a small hand pump connected to the outside well. Mom gave my little brother baths in that sink, mixing water heated on the stove with the water from the pump. As we got older, of course, we bathed in large washtubs, and if we were really lucky, it would rain and we could bathe outside behind the back porch, as the rain would have all gathered into one area of the roof and run off in a great torrent.

There was a pantry just off the kitchen with shelves for canned food and a pie safe with two doors and six tin panels with the characteristic small patterned holes to let air in but keep the bugs out. We spent most of our time in the kitchen, usually around the stove since it was the home's primary heat source, and the kitchen was where the family would sit around the table and visit. Sometimes my brother and I would churn the milk by using the dasher (plunger) in the glazed and fired clay churn to make clabber and whey, which in some fashion my grandmother would turn into other things such as butter and buttermilk.

There was a back porch out of the kitchen across which the long middle hall could be reached. There was a table built into the wall on the porch where we kept a bucket with water from the pump and a gourd, and later a dipper, with which to drink the fresh water. Then on the left side of the long hall were three bedrooms, and my brother and I slept in the front bedroom with a door to Mom and Dad's room and a separate door out to the front porch.

To me the most interesting thing about this old home, built by my granddaddy in 1890, was that he had to cut the trees from the spot where he wanted to build the house, and the stumps of those trees were still under the house! The house rested upon brick pillars at the corners and at several places along each side, but there was no foundation as such, and the entire underside of the home was open. So instead of having the dogs "trot" up and down the long central hall to stay out of the weather (such as was the case with many of our neighbors), our dogs stayed under the house. Right there with the chickens, cats, and an occasional copperhead snake!

Outside we had a smokehouse with a pigsty attached. My brother and I were given the duty of "slopping the hogs" every day, which meant throwing a bucket full of table scraps and kernel corn into a trough for them. The kernel corn came from ears of corn that we had shucked and run through a "grinder," which had separated the kernels of corn from the cob. The hogs were slaughtered every November, and the meat would be smoked in the smokehouse, hanging on hooks from the rafters, prior to being taken into the house. There was a very large kettle in the dirt floor of the smokehouse where the fire would be controlled, contained and safe.

The ears of corn were stored in a separate outbuilding to the rear of the twenty-acre "home place," and that is where we would shuck the ears and grind the kernels for the pigs and hogs. The corn was grown in a separate twenty-acre parcel adjacent to the "home place." I remember my dad and my granddaddy plowing the cornfield with the horse that we had. And, of course, we had a milk cow, which I was pretty good at milking. It really was not easy at first, because if the cow did not like the way a person was pulling on her udders, she had a way of kicking the milk pail away! And that was not a very efficient way to get the milk inside the house. I guess one could accurately say that a bond of sorts had to be established with the cow before the job could be done well.

We had lots of chickens, and the important thing was to not become "attached" to them— that is, to begin to think of them as pets or anything like that. And I say that for the very simple reason that I would always get a little queasy whenever one of the grown-ups would get one of them ready for Sunday dinner. That always meant snapping their heads off and watching them flutter and flop around the yard for five or ten minutes without their heads while they died!

We had a privy (a "three holer" with the attendant Sears Roebuck catalog and sack of lime), which, of course, everyone in the country had to have back then before anyone had electricity and running water in their homes. When I got a little older, I would have to accompany my grandmother out to the privy at night before she went to bed, and I would carry our .22-caliber target pistol to guard against the snakes. I remember killing two copperheads over the years. One thing about the privy that was a little unsettling to the uninitiated was that my granddaddy had learned that the land just behind the privy—and the lime—was the best place for growing our tomatoes.

Right outside the window of my mom's and dad's bedroom was a chinaberry tree. That in itself was not very important. But what was important is that my brother and I entertained ourselves for hours on end watching the robins eat the berries. The robins, all of them, would then (for lack of a better term) become drunk, as they would wobble around and try to fly only to crash beak first into the grass! And when they reached the point of realizing they had eaten too much, they would lie in the grass until they sobered up!

Growing up in the country was a great experience. Sure, my brother, Donnie, and I had to walk to town to be with some of our friends when we were little and before we got bicycles, but we knew so much more about how the "real world" worked than all of them put together.

—BARRY SWITZER, Former football coach
Hometown: Crosset, Arkansas

{Gregory Vasquez}

I cannot think of the house I grew up in without thinking of my mother, Juana Tovar Vasquez. My father died before I was five years old but not before he and my mother had two more sons. Widowed, barely able to speak English, my mother spent her life working to give me and my brothers the footing to stand tall and prosper in America.

My mother was from a rural part of Mexico, brought to the United States by my father to start a new life. She had every reason to go back to Mexico after my father died—she was in a foreign country whose language she didn't know, with a limited education; she had left a son and daughter behind in Mexico; and her brothers and sisters were still there. She did take us to Mexico to visit once or twice, but never considered staying because she knew we could build a better life here in the States.

The house she raised us in was more than fifty years old when I was born. It had electricity but no indoor plumbing, no running water, no furnace, and certainly no air conditioning. Our source of water was an indoor well and our bathroom was an outhouse.

Our house sat on a large lot with a couple of big oak trees and a smaller elm tree or two. It was two stories tall and all wood, with a back porch and an earthen basement. Separate from the house were three sheds: one for coal, one for chickens, and one for miscellaneous items. From the back porch we could see our garden, the outhouse, and our "woods"—a small, tree-filled area nearby with a narrow creek running through it.

Our lives played out on the first floor of the house; we used the upstairs for some storage, but it sat largely empty. The truth is, I never felt comfortable upstairs, perhaps because it was the setting for my mother's frightening stories and my half-brother Natchio's sword and war relic collections. It was also impossible to control the temperatures up there—sweltering hot in the summer and bitterly cold in the winter.

Newton was a manufacturing town; the major employer was the Maytag Company. It was then and remains today a predominantly white community, where our family and a handful of others composed the tiny Mexican population. It was not until years later that I realized that my father and other Mexican men of his age were the last of the men that the Rock Island Railroad brought north to build and expand the railroad. Those men simply never returned home after the work was complete. Many of them eventually moved to Des Moines, which was much larger and had a more significant Mexican population.

An illustration of our house in Iowa.

GREGORY VASQUEZ

Our house was located in an industrial area sandwiched between the Vernon Company (a coal company), the Newton foundry (a dump), and the railroad tracks. The Vernon Company also had a small waste outlet and the city had a storm sewer that emptied to the south of our home. The water waste created a marsh area that froze in the winter and became our very own skating pond. Every once in a while we would smell an unpleasant odor—but it also meant we had our own ice skating rink!

Our home was bordered by a dirt road on one side and a cinder-topped road on the other. When the traffic on these roads was fast and heavy, it would kick up constant clouds of dust. When it rained, the traffic on the dirt road struggled to go up or down, vehicles swerving from side to side trying not to slide into the ditch. The close-by railroad tracks handled heavy train traffic, so there was no escaping the shrieking train whistles.

Newton didn't have public transportation, so we walked everywhere we went—school, church, the grocery store. There was a taxi cab company but we could never afford to use it. We would pull a wagon to the Farmers Super Market to tote our food home. On occasion, the owner would bring the groceries back for us.

To the west of our home was a family with seven children and neither parent employed. They were probably the first white people my brothers and I ever met, and they gave us our first exposure to English, which I didn't speak until kindergarten. Gary, whose dad collected scrap metal and sold it to earn extra cash, taught us to collect scrap metal and pop bottles for money. Sometimes his dad would buy it from us, and other times we would drag it to the foundry and sell it ourselves. And to the north was the magnificent home of a Mexican family that had done quite well; we always knew that anyone could make it in America if they were given the chance.

But our home was best of all. That house was our nest, and my mother the queen bird, doing all she could to make a better life for us. I remember peeking out from underneath the covers on cold winter mornings and seeing my mother trying to get a fire started to warm up part of the house. More often than not the room would fill up with smoke—but the smell meant things were about to warm up!

We didn't celebrate birthdays and there were no gifts at Christmas, so our holiday celebrations were with food around the table, which my mother labored over. She was always glued to the kitchen, filling the house with the smell of tortillas, pinto beans, and sopa de arrozo, cooking and roasting hot peppers on the stove to be ground into a side dish of salsa. We had a propane stove but she preferred the wood-burning oven. During holidays, she would place the turkey or ham on the oil-burning heater to finish cooking. To this day, I have never tasted better turkey or ham.

Our house was a place of security; it was literally all we owned, but it was more than enough—because it wasn't all we had. We had our mother's love, and we had her dreams for our lives—which made us all the more diligent about making those dreams come true.

I spent four years in the U.S. Navy and after an honorable discharge, I used my military benefits to attend and graduate from the University of Iowa. I also found Cherry, the love of my life and wife of thirty-nine years, and we had three children, Angie, Tricia, and Sorral. Like me, Cherry is of Mexican parents and a poor background. Together, we are committed to making a better life for our daughters, just like my mother did for us. Throughout my life I have been especially sensitive to the struggle of single mothers, children growing up poor, the difficulty of language barriers. My mother never let these things stop her from building a loving home, starting in the kitchen.

—GREGORY VASQUEZ, Field auditor
Hometown: Newton, Iowa

{ Vera Wang }

Of all the homes I have lived in during my fifty-six years, each has held a special place in my heart and my memory. But my favorite has to be my parents' home in Pound Ridge, New York, because it embodied so many of our family's hopes and desires and a lot of love. My father, Cheng Ching Wang, and my mother, Florence Wu Wang, both left lives of privilege and prominence in China to settle in the United States just before the Communist revolution, and like many immigrants before them, they fully embraced the spirit and ideals of their newly adopted country.

After twenty-five years, my father, who had by then built a successful international trading company, decided to acquire a weekend home for us outside of the city. The long, exhaustive search for this new house provided nearly as much fun and excitement as the reality of owning a second home. In the end, we lost a lovely house on its own pond to a higher bidder, so my father decided to build . . . and with that end in mind purchased thirty pristine acres with a thirteen-acre private lake in the same little hamlet of New York State.

For kids who had grown up in the city, this unique property was like a private nature reserve. There were woods to trample through, hills to climb, fish to catch, and a lake to swim in or paddle a boat on. But most of all, to my parents, particularly my father (though he never actually expressed it in words), this home symbolized so much more. He had been able to survive a revolution, leave his roots behind, and provide for his family in a whole new world.

I was twenty-three years old at the time and working as an editor at *Vogue* magazine when my father enlisted me to work on designing the house and landscaping the grounds with architect George Van Geldern and builder Vito Fossella. And amazingly enough, from the very start there seemed to be one singular artistic vision, which rarely happens in a creative project. The house would embody the beauty, simplicity, and tranquillity of a Japanese teahouse. Eventually, there would be a changing pavilion by the pool and a tennis court built into the rocks. There was also a tiny waterfall and a dam on the property where we would all "picnic" often. My father later added a caretaker's home and fifty more acres to the property.

But aside from the overwhelming physical beauty of our place—it was the warmth, love, and happiness we all shared together with our dearest friends, relatives, and one another. Thanksgivings with my mother's wonderful huge buffets and skating on the frozen lake over

Christmas, summers spent swimming, playing tennis, rowing, and biking, and, of course, more food, cookouts, Chinese dinners, and always birthdays.

But life as we once knew it had to move on, and like everything else, our home, once filled with such joy, optimism, and life, now sits beautifully, though quietly, alone. It is hard to find the time to get up there; my husband and I work late on Friday evenings, our daughters are involved in their after-school activities, and my mother, who adored this home, died in 2004 after being infirm for several years.

Our place in Pound Ridge will always represent a true appreciation for nature, a profound love of family, and a deep love of life. Often, when I am traveling all over the world and busy dealing with my own family, my business, and my life, I think of Pound Ridge and the true happiness I experienced there. More than any one room, place, or location, be it a cottage or a mansion, a home represents an idealized dream of our most intimate life. It can also reflect our state of mind, our innermost emotions, and our need for safety, refuge, and comfort.

Pound Ridge will always mean all that for me.

—VERA WANG, Clothing designer
Hometown: Pound Ridge, New York

My parents' house in Pound Ridge, New York.

{Rick Warren}

In traveling around the world, I've been invited
into thousands of homes—from mud huts to mansions, from shacks and shanties to skyscrapers,
from cottages and chalets to castles. I've slept in adobes, tents, trailers, houseboats, log cabins,
lean-tos, and too many other dwellings to count. What I've noticed is that where people live
affects how they live. As Churchill said, "We shape our buildings and they shape us." If you lived
for a month in a brownstone then spent another one living in a mobile home, you'd likely notice
some major changes in your habits.

Growing up, my family lived in several different houses, but the one that shaped me most
was the one I lived in from fifth grade until I completed high school ('66 to '72). My older brother
had already moved out to go to college, so there were five of us—my mom and dad, my younger
sister, and my grandmother—but we had guests in our home almost daily.

Our house was located in Redwood Valley, a laid-back and spread-out rural community (35
square miles) two hours north of San Francisco in Northern California. It was a picturesque setting of redwood trees, pastures, pear orchards, and grape vineyards, with the Russian River
bisecting the valley.

Many of my neighbors moved to this quiet area of Mendocino County to start small, family-
owned vineyards in the area's fertile soil and the protected climate, which was perfect for growing
wine grapes. In the 1960s, before California wines became famous, no one had heard of Fetzer or
Frey or Weibel wines, but their kids were my friends and classmates.

The population of Redwood Valley was only about 500 when I lived there, and we were
spread out. There was no center, except for a tiny general store with a single gas pump in front.
The nearest town was Ukiah (population 8,000) nine miles south, where we went to high school,
and where my mother was a school librarian. My father, a minister, supervised a dozen small
churches in Mendocino and Lake counties that could not afford full-time pastors.

We lived on a ten-acre lot, with four distinct sections: our house was surrounded with oak,
redwood, and pine trees. Across our creek was an area Dad had cleared for an acre of vegetable
garden and fruit trees. The back area was pasture where there was an old barn, and where we
sometimes kept a couple of cows. But the jewel of it all was the one-acre pond set about 50 yards
from our back door. Oh, that pond!

In many ways, I enjoyed a Huck Finn childhood centered around that body of water: swimming, fishing, diving, frog-gigging, rope-swinging over the water, playing on our two wooden rafts, and catching tadpoles were all a regular part of growing up. That pond spelled fun! Dad put up an old army tent on the backside of the pond for my "club-house," and I promptly filled it with a cot, a transistor radio, and stacks of comic books. I still remember the smell of that hot canvas on a summer day. My winter hangout was the tree fort in a giant oak.

Our house in Redwood Valley, California.

Redwood Valley was a wonderful, relaxed place to grow up. It offered winding back roads for bicycling, the Russian River, and plenty of places to explore. One favorite was to walk the nearby railroad tracks, shooting stuff with a pellet rifle. In the summer, we'd climb down into the creek bed and pick huge blackberries that had ripened slowly in the shade.

Things were pretty sleepy in Redwood Valley until a flamboyant "religious prophet" moved in with a bunch of families from back East and started a new "church" that had all the classic signs of a religious cult. Our nearest neighbors were members. The group grew rapidly and soon a dozen buses filled with "city people" from the San Francisco Bay area were arriving in Redwood Valley each weekend to attend the People's Temple. Their leader, Jim Jones, later led the group to move to Guyana to form a utopian community, where, in 1978, more than 900 people died in the largest mass murder/suicide in U.S. history. I lost a number of childhood friends who drank the Kool-Aid in the South American jungle. That event made me vow to expose religious fraud anytime I find it.

I remember many of the features of our house in Redwood Valley. First, it was always getting larger. Dad, an incessant builder, who built more than 150 church buildings in his lifetime, was always improving our home or adding on to it. He doubled the size over the years, turned the detached garage into a home for my grandmother, and built a two-story addition.

One of the first improvements he made was to tear out the wall on the side of the house that faced the pond and install a massive floor-to-ceiling bay window that ran the length of our living

The pond near our house where
I used to play as a child.

room. It filled our home with light and gave an indoor/outdoor feel that magnified the beauty of the surrounding nature rather than the home itself. Now, forty years later, I pastor a church that has two walls made completely of glass looking out on God's creation, and our home's living room has an entire wall of glass so you can look out on an canyon that is an Audubon wildlife sanctuary with a pond. I wonder where I got that idea?

Our home in Redwood Valley had two sources of heat. First, it had a very large fireplace, where Dad would build a roaring fire on cold mornings. Often it was the smell of that fire that acted as an alarm clock, telling my body to wake up. Second, hot water pipes ran through the cement slab foundation so the floors were always warm even when the rooms weren't. It made lying on the floor watching TV quite comfortable! From my travels, I've learned to appreciate what a wonderful gift a warm house really is.

My bedroom had a door to the outside, and I could come and go without going through the rest of the house. As a teenager, this was convenient. Most of the year I left my door open all night, so I could hear the bullfrogs croaking from the pond through the screen. Although my room was small it was crammed with all the things I was interested in: my collections of shells, rocks, coins, stamps, books, wishbones, horseshoes, and assorted other collections, including forty-two years of *National Geographic*. It also housed my two guitars, a fender amp, and a homemade recording studio.

Attached to my bedroom was a half-bathroom with a sink and toilet. My folks allowed me to paint it fluorescent green and then write one-liners, both wise and funny, in black graffiti style all over the walls. One that I remember was "Not to decide is to decide." When guests used my bedroom, you could often hear them laugh as they lay down on my bed and looked up, seeing additional sayings spray painted on my ceiling.

The center of activity inside our house was not the living room, but the kitchen. It was always full of delicious smells and happy sounds. Mom was an extraordinary cook, who could whip up literally anything. It didn't matter if it was cooking for a dozen of my friends, or a hundred people that dad had just invited over after a meeting. She loved the challenge. (In the '80s and '90s, Mom cooked for thousands of relief workers, while Dad led rebuilding teams at disaster sites all around the world. They modeled our purpose-driven global P.E.A.C.E. plan long before we launched it.)

Because our family loved fellowship, hospitality, fun, and food, the most important piece of furniture in our home was THE DINING ROOM TABLE. This was no wimpy mass-produced store model. No sir! It was hand-logged and custom cut from a giant sequoia redwood that had fallen in a forest on a friend's land near Comptche. It was a single, solid piece of glazed redwood, twelve feet long, five feet wide, and four inches thick, with enormous redwood legs. The table filled and dominated the room, and once set in place was impossible to move because of its weight.

Both Mom and Dad had the cheerful gift of hospitality and believed in following Romans 12:13 "When God's children are in need, be the one to help them out. And get into the habit of inviting guests home for dinner or, if they need lodging, for the night" *(New Living Translation)*. Once my dad added up the number of guests my mom had fed in our home that single year, and it totaled over 2,000. So growing up, I never knew who else would show up at that giant table for breakfast. But I learned that loving hospitality turns a house into a home.

Because of all the meals and memories made around that table, all the fascinating people I met, and all the enlightening conversations I heard growing up while sitting there, that table, which is now in my possession, represents all that was good about growing up as a Warren.

I began this piece by pointing out that our shelters shape us. Our place influences our perspective. It's certainly been true in my own life. Growing up in our rural Redwood Valley home taught me to value the natural over artificial, the simple over the complex, light instead of darkness, the outdoors over indoors, informality over formality, and trust over caution. Today, just as my parents greeted everyone with warmth and open arms, Kay and I have sought to create a home and a church that make people feel welcomed and wanted, regardless of their background. That hospitality is motivated by the Good News that God is preparing an eternal home in heaven for everyone who will trust in His grace and His Son, regardless of their background.

— RICK WARREN, Pastor
Hometown: Redwood Valley, California

RICK WARREN

{Viola Wert}

For me, home was the place I could keep coming back to and always feel comfortable. I felt so comfortable, in fact, that I refused to ever really leave. I lived in this house nestled in Lynnville, a small village northwest of Allentown, Pennsylvania, from the day I was born in 1909 until 1911, again from 1915 to 1918, and then again in 1942, when I stayed for good. My grandparents first owned the home, then my father. In the early years, my grandparents, parents, two brothers, and two sisters all lived there. During the years I was away, I still spent summers at the house. Now I have been there continuously for the past sixty-three years, by myself.

The home was originally built in 1869 for a Lutheran pastor, Reverend Henry Fegley. The fairly large, white-framed house has three rooms and a pantry on the first floor, three rooms with closets on the second floor, and an attic on the third floor. Since our family arrived there, we've made plenty of changes: there have been porches and a sunroom added, and at some point in the early 1900s a study on the second floor was turned into a bathroom; but for the most part the house stands as it has since 1932, with me in it.

My mother and grandmother used to take over the kitchen, cooking and baking away for the whole family. The farm got noisy at times, with all the animals and work to be done. We kept a "house" cow to produce our milk supply and several chickens for our eggs. There were horses in the barn and plenty of kitties scattered over the property.

The town of Lynnville is a collection of all the typical buildings: a church on the hill, a hotel, a store, a school, a fire company, and several houses. An article written for Allentown's main newspaper, *Morning Call*, says that in 1960 there were thirty-two residents in the village and that the population had not varied more than four or five in the previous hundred years. Around that time, a sign was painted onto the side of a barn at the Lynnville Hotel, providing a perfect description of Lynnville: "Biggest Little Village in America: 1 Hotel, 1 Store, 1 Garage, 1 Fire Company, 1 Doctor, 1 Lawyer [my father], 1 Justice of the Peace [my brother], and 1 Industrial Company." Although it was little, we had all we needed, and that barn even attracted a good bit of tourism, people driving through and stopping to take pictures.

The wonderful part of such a "big little village" with one of everything is that we were isolated but self-sufficient. Every family knew the others, and they all relied on one another, to some extent, for survival. Most of the food came from the neighboring farms or the families

Our family home in Lynnville, Pennsylvania.

VIOLA WERT

The Lynnville Hotel.

themselves. And because we knew everyone, we trusted everyone. There was no crime, not even the fleeting thought of danger. Everyone went to church together, celebrated births and marriages together, and mourned deaths together. Our lives were intertwined.

The men would often meet at the store to grab the newspaper and trade neighborhood news, while the women would tend to the children, plan church events, and feed their families. Our community was a whole, not just the sum of its parts. We helped one another, for example, when someone fell ill or came on hard times. We served the community by helping at the church, volunteering at the fire company, and hosting rallies in the picnic grove at the firehouse. And we served the country, too, lending men to the armed forces to fight in several wars.

Whenever I returned home, after a long day or a couple of months away, someone in the family was always there to welcome me, whether to offer support or to catch me up on local news and gossip. I suppose that's how I knew I could always come back without missing a beat. I remember how cherished our Christmases were, the whole town gathering together at church and then just our family gathering together at home. And it's not just an old wives' tale that children who misbehave get lumps of coal in their stocking—we really did. The tradition in our family was that kids who were good received oranges and candy, but those who weren't got coal.

The central spot in the house was the kitchen, where all of the activity took place: cooking and baking, eating and entertaining, sewing and making soap. We'd sit around and discuss everything there and make all the family decisions. The deep connection to my community and family that was fostered in my early days at home may be why my roots are too strong to pull up.

My parents encouraged me to pursue higher education, and I did. I earned a master's degree and certification as a principal and had a forty-six-year career in education. I taught from 1928 to 1974, and then I advanced to become principal of an entire school, at a time when careers for women were few. I was able to encourage my students as I had been encouraged and create a real community in the classroom.

I understood by example the power of working together, because that was the spirit of the home and the town and the time that shaped my life. I hope I have passed some of that on to the hundreds of children whose lives I was given the honor to shape, even a little, myself.

—VIOLA WERT, Retired school principal
Hometown: Lynnville, Pennsylvania

{Acknowledgments}

The acknowledgments for a book about home can only start in one place for me—with my parents. They started with nothing and gave me everything, and I will always be grateful for the home they built for my brother, my sister, and me, with their love, their values, and their example.

I want to thank the hundreds of people over the course of my career as a lawyer who placed their trust in my hands when the homes they had so carefully built were tested by tragedy.

I want to thank the countless Americans, starting with my friends and neighbors in North Carolina, who invited me and Elizabeth into their homes, shared their lives with us, and fought by our side to change this country.

I want to thank my daughter Cate and my friend Jonathan Prince, whose work with me and with all the participants in this book helped to bring our homes to life on these pages. And I want to thank my friend Harrison Hickman, whose original insight into the power the memory of first homes has for so many people helped to inspire this book.

I want to thank Bob Barnett as well as everyone at HarperCollins—Jane Friedman, Joe Tessitore, Kathy Huck-Seymour, Paul Olsewski, Ryu Spaeth, Leah Carlson-Stanisic, Howard Klein, Diane Aronson, Karen Lumley, and Donna Ruvituso—all of whom believed in this book from the very first discussion.

I want to thank all of my friends, advisers, and staff who helped to make this project work—Alexis Bar, Nick Baldick, Josh Brumberger, Peter Eskra, David Ginsberg, Lori Krause, Miles Lackey, Dan Lander, Jenni Lee, Kathleen McGlynn, David Medina, Kim Rubey, Peter Scher, and Jennifer Swanson.

Above all, I want to thank my wife, Elizabeth, and our four children—Wade, Cate, Emma Claire, and Jack. Wherever I am, you are home.